Indira Gandhi Speaks

Indira Gandhi Speaks ON DEMOCRACY, SOCIALISM, AND THIRD WORLD NONALIGNMENT

Edited, and with an Introduction, by
HENRY M. CHRISTMAN

Taplinger Publishing Company · New York

DS 407
G29
1975

First Edition

Published in the United States in 1975 by
TAPLINGER PUBLISHING CO., INC.
New York, New York

Copyright © 1975 by Henry M. Christman
All rights reserved. Printed in the U.S.A.

No part of this book may be reproduced or transmitted in any
form or by any means, electronic or mechanical, including
photocopy, recording, or any information storage and retrieval
system now known or to be invented, without permission in
writing from the publisher, except by a reviewer who wishes
to quote brief passages in connection with a review written for
inclusion in a magazine, newspaper, or broadcast.

Published simultaneously in the Dominion of Canada by
Burns & MacEachern, Ltd., Toronto

Library of Congress Catalog Card Number: 72-6611

ISBN 0-8008-4180-8

Designed by Mollie M. Torras

Contents

Introduction

India warrants close and continuing international attention for many reasons. It is one of the major population centers of the world. It is a leader in the Third World nonalignment movement seeking to avoid domination by the major power blocs. It is the center of one of the world's great historic civilizations, with a remarkable multicultural, multireligious society in transition. And it is the world's largest democracy.

That Indian democracy has survived to this point of history is due in large part to Prime Minister Indira Gandhi, who has had the foresight to recognize the economic, social and political problems that could bring about the collapse of her country, and has endeavored to meet and solve those problems within the structure of parliamentary democracy.

Indira Priyadarshini Nehru Gandhi, the daughter of Jawaharlal Nehru and Kamala Kaul Nehru, was born on November 19, 1917, in Allahabad, northern India, in the mansion of her grandfather, Motilal Nehru, a successful attorney and prominent leader in the Indian independence movement. The Nehru home, which Motilal Nehru named Anand Bhavan, the Abode of Joy, was a beehive of political activity; it served as a meeting place, and, in later years, an official headquarters, for the Indian National Congress, the organized independence force. During Indira's childhood, it even functioned as an emergency hospital for Congress demonstrators injured by police.

7

The key strategy of the Indian independence movement was *satyagraha,* or nonviolent disobedience, a carefully planned, disciplined, continuing campaign of peaceful protest advocated and directed by Mohandas K. Gandhi. Motilal and Jawaharlal Nehru were leaders, strategists and active participants in the independence movement, and, consequently, were repeatedly jailed.

Indira Nehru's formal schooling was sporadic, but she was tutored by her family, her horizons were widened by contact with the distinguished visitors to Anand Bhavan, and she read widely and voraciously in the extensive family library. At the age of eight, she was taken abroad on a European stay that lasted almost two years, during which she accompanied her father in meeting many of the foremost intellectuals and political leaders of the Continent.

In 1930, Gandhi launched a nationwide campaign of civil disobedience directed against the colonial government's monopoly on the making of salt. Young Indira was then twelve years old; excluded from active participation in the disobedience drive because of her youth, she proceeded to found a youth auxiliary, known as the "Monkey Brigade," which served the Congress Party leaders and demonstrators as first-aid attendants, cooks, water bearers and messengers.

Early in 1931, Indira's grandfather, Motilal, died; and in 1936, her mother, Kamala. Indira grew even closer to her father, Jawaharlal; and even when they were separated by his imprisonment, he directed her development through letters.

During this period, Indira's formal education broadened into new spheres. In 1934, she entered Visva-Bharati University, the cultural institution founded and headed by the Indian poet and intellectual, Rabindranath Tagore. While there, she came to know Tagore personally, and on various occasions has referred to him as one of the great influences in her life.

Subsequently, Indira entered Somerville College, Oxford. In Oxford and in London, she associated with fellow students from other British colonies and with activists of the British political Left, taking part in various anticolonial and anti-Fascist campaigns.

In 1941, Indira was back in India to stay; and in March 1942, she married Feroze Gandhi, who, despite the name, was not related to the internationally famous Mohandas K. Gandhi. Indira's family were Brahmins, originally from Kashmir; Feroze's family were Parsees, Zoroastrian in religion, originally from Persia. They had been childhood friends, and later fellow students together at Oxford, and both belonged to the modernist, politically progressive wing of the independence movement. But for Indira to marry not only out of caste, but even outside the Hindu religion, was shocking and scandalous to orthodox Hindus.

Both Indira and Feroze Gandhi were soon in prison for their activities on behalf of Indian independence. Indira was detained for thirteen months. Upon release, she reentered independence movement activities, on occasion working under the personal direction of Mohandas Gandhi.

August 1947 brought independence to India, but not in the form sought by the Nehru family; the subcontinent was partitioned into the independent nations of India and Pakistan, the latter an explicitly Moslem state. Partition caused one of the greatest migrations in world history, as Moslems fled into the new nation of Pakistan, while Hindus fled outward into India.

Jawaharlal Nehru became the first Prime Minister of independent India, and Indira Gandhi moved with him into the official residence of the Prime Minister, not only to act as official hostess, but also as Nehru's trusted assistant and confidante.

The historic crisscross migration between India and Pakistan was only one of the overwhelming problems facing Nehru; the two states had no more than attained independence than they were at war over Kashmir, the ancestral home region of the Nehrus in northern India. In addition to fighting a two-front war against both West and East Pakistan, and receiving millions of destitute, desperate refugees, Nehru also was faced with critical economic problems and turbulent outbreaks among the Indian masses. A tragic climax was reached with the assassination of Mohandas Gandhi by a Hindu fanatic in 1948.

An uneasy peace was brought about between India and Pakistan that same year through a cease-fire supervised by the United Nations. With fighting terminated, Nehru was able to focus on constructive national and international matters. During the following years, Nehru, with Indira Gandhi at his side, took India's cause and concerns to various world centers, including an official visit to the United States.

Mrs. Gandhi's family life also deepened during these years. A son, Rajiv, born before independence, had been joined by a second son, Sanjay. Feroze Gandhi had meanwhile developed his own political career, winning election to India's national Parliament.

It must be remembered that Nehru was not only a statesman but a politician as well, and that the entire Nehru family had taken active roles in the Indian National Congress independence movement; and when, after independence, the Indian National Congress evolved into a political party, the Congress Party, Nehru and Indira Gandhi took leadership roles in Congress politics. In 1959, Indira Gandhi was elected President of the Congress Party. Thus came about the remarkable circumstances of the Nehru family holding formal leadership of both government and party simultaneously.

In her one-year term as President of the Congress Party, Mrs. Gandhi took the initiative on two controversial issues, and prevailed on both. As a result of her response to local aspirations, the State of Bombay was divided into two new states on the basis of language. The State of Kerala presented an even more controversial matter, as that state was then headed by a Communist government voted into power through free elections. Mrs. Gandhi was in the forefront of successful efforts to unseat the Kerala Communist government in midterm.

By 1962, India was in a second war, this time with China, as a result of Chinese invasion of Indian territory. Nehru, who had befriended the People's Republic of China, was deeply disillusioned by the Chinese attack. Although the actual war was of short duration, its effect took a heavy toll on Nehru, who rapidly declined in health. In May 1964, Jawaharlal Nehru, first Prime Minister of India, died.

This period brought great personal burdens for Mrs. Gandhi. In 1960, her husband had died, leaving her with their two young sons; then she cared for her father throughout his illness until his death in 1964.

Nehru was succeeded as Prime Minister by Lal Bahadur Shastri. Mrs. Gandhi entered the Government as Minister of Information and Broadcasting, meanwhile winning election to Parliament. She endeavored to modernize and streamline the ministerial bureaucracy, and took special interest in the development of television.

In April 1965, there were border skirmishes between India and Pakistan, and by September they were at war. As a result of this second outbreak of hostilities between India and Pakistan since their independence, the Soviet Union proposed mediation. In January 1966, Prime Minister Shastri and President Ayub Khan of Pakistan signed an accord in Tashkent; and, only hours later, Shastri died as a result of the strain of negotiations.

Indira Gandhi was elected as leader of the Congress Parliamentary Party on January 19, 1966, and was sworn into office as Prime Minister on January 24. She followed up her inauguration by making visits to London, Moscow, and the United States, and became the first female head of government ever to visit Washington.

In her first year as Prime Minister, Mrs. Gandhi was confronted with major domestic problems. The rupee had to be devalued by more than one-half; riots over the division of Punjab into two new states rocked India, with mobs turned back with force at the doors of Parliament; and, most serious of all, there were food shortages that almost became a catastrophic famine.

February 1967 saw India's fourth general election since independence. The Congress Party majority in Parliament was substantially reduced, and opposition parties came into power in several state governments.

This election revealed the basic structural weakness of the Congress Party as a political entity. The roots of the party were in the independence movement, which had brought together a disparate coalition united against the British colonialist regime. As a political party, however, the Congress Party lacked cohesion; and with Nehru gone, it was increasingly vulnerable to inroads from both the political Right and the political Left.

Mrs. Gandhi was determined to lead the party toward a more clearly defined secularist and socialist policy and image. Her first major opportunity came in 1967, with the retirement of Sarvepalli Radhakrishnan from the ceremonial office of President of the Republic. Radhakrishnan had previously served as Vice-President, and had succeeded to the Presidency without opposition upon the retirement of India's first President, Rajendra Prasad. Under ordinary circumstances, the then Vice-President, Zakir Husain, would have succeeded Radhakrishnan to the Presidency as a matter of course. But orthodox Hindus asserted that Husain, a Moslem, or any other non-Hindu should not be President of the Republic.

The political battle lines were drawn. Was India a Hindu society in which all the minorities were relegated to second-class status; or was India a secular, egalitarian democracy? Mrs. Gandhi insisted that India was and must be the latter. She placed her entire power and prestige behind Husain, and he triumphed in a hard-fought election.

During 1967, India was again threatened by serious food shortages. Once again, famine was narrowly averted, this time the feat accomplished with large-scale assistance from the United States.

Nineteen sixty-seven was notable in still another respect: the increasing influence of both parliamentary and revolutionary Communism. The Communists returned to power in Kerala on the crest of a major electoral victory, and they also came to power temporarily through a coalition government in the key state of West Bengal.

The most dramatic development, however, took place in the small village of Naxalbari, where revolutionary Communists incited peasants to seize land, execute landlords and set up a commune. The revolutionary commune of Naxalbari was short-lived; the uprising was rapidly suppressed by governmental forces. "Naxalite" entered the international political lexicon as a term denoting a Maoist-type, conspiratorial Communist plotting and inciting violent revolution of the underprivileged.

Mrs. Gandhi grew increasingly dissatisfied with the inability of the Congress Party to cope effectively with the drastic problems facing India and with the ominous dissatisfaction and unrest among the people. In 1969, the death of President Husain touched off a power struggle between Mrs. Gandhi and the party political bosses, popularly known as "the syndicate." Mrs. Gandhi resolutely pressed both her governmental and political goals; in July 1969, she secured the nationalization of banking in India, and in August 1969, her candidate for President of the nation, V. V. Giri, defeated the candidate of "the syndicate." The Congress Party then openly split in two, with a number of Congress parliamentary deputies formally joining the parliamentary opposition. The defection of the more conservative Congress deputies left the Gandhi Government in a parliamentary minority, dependent upon the votes of opposition parties. In March 1971, a special election was held, in advance of the expiration of the Government's term of office. The New Congress Party led by Mrs. Gandhi swept to a landslide victory, winning an absolute parliamentary majority.

Greatly bolstered by her victory, Prime Minister Gandhi was soon to face an international crisis of historic proportion. Shortly before democratic India had held elections, Pakistan had also held elections, the latter scheduled to restore civilian government after a dozen years of military rule. The Awami League, a Bengali nationalist party led by Sheikh Mujibur Rahman, swept to a landslide victory in populous East Pakistan, thereby winning an absolute majority in what was scheduled to be Pakistan's new national parliament.

Accordingly, the military government of Pakistan should have called upon Sheikh Mujibur Rahman to lead the new civilian government. But Pakistan's military strongman, President Yahya Khan, distrusted the Awami League program for Bengali autonomy. Yahya Khan delayed convening of the new national assembly; rioting and strikes resulted in East Pakistan; and in March 1971, Yahya Khan ordered the Pakistani Army to crush the supporters of Mujibur Rahman.

What had been an East Pakistan autonomy movement promptly became a Bengali independence movement. The Pakistani Army imposed a ruthless military occupation on East Pakistan, and millions of refugees poured across the borders into India. Pakistan rejected India's protests, and, in December 1971, Pakistan attacked India. India quickly defeated Pakistan, and East Pakistan was liberated, becoming the new nation of Bangladesh.

The result was a historic shift of power in the Indian subcontinent. The old Pakistan, India's traditional rival, had been transformed into two separate nations, the most populous of which, Bangladesh, was India's new friend. Prime Minister Gandhi had triumphed again.

Meanwhile, Mrs. Gandhi had further solidified India's position by signing a Treaty of Peace, Friendship and Cooperation with the

U.S.S.R. in August 1971. By this move, India and the Soviet Union formalized their goal to restrict and neutralize the Asian influence of the People's Republic of China.

On May 18, 1974, India took a pioneering step forward by exploding a nuclear device underground, thus becoming the world's sixth nuclear power. Replying to international reaction, Prime Minister Gandhi stated:

> I am aware that in popular parlance nuclear explosion evokes an awesome and horrifying picture. However, this is because our minds have been conditioned by misuse of nuclear energy for the development of weapons, and by the use of these weapons in Hiroshima and Nagasaki. We in India have condemned and will continue to condemn military uses of nuclear energy as a threat to humanity. Development of peaceful uses of nuclear energy, rather than posing a threat, provides a ray of hope for mankind, faced as it is by the specter of dwindling energy resources.

Under Prime Minister Gandhi's leadership, the Indian nuclear program has two declared goals: generation of cheap electrical power; and utilization of atomic energy for improvements in agriculture, industry, medicine, and other fields.

As the Prime Minister's biographer, Trevor Drieberg, wrote of her recently, "Mrs. Gandhi is today on a political pinnacle where she holds absolute power and could, if she wanted, do without the party . . . she has achieved this by purely democratic, parliamentary processes . . . she is there by the people's unfettered will, expressed through free elections. She is a political phenomenon, in a class by herself. Her sanction is the people. Their votes put her in power despite the attempts of various elite groups to see that she was shut out of its portals."

This book does not presume to be a definitive work on Indira Gandhi, on India, or on Third World issues. It does, however, serve as an introduction to each and all of these subjects. In the first section, Mrs. Gandhi speaks on a variety of domestic issues that far transcend Indian affairs; indeed, these are the problems that face the developing nations and regions of the world. In the second section, Mrs. Gandhi defines India's international perspective. Finally, she speaks of political and intellectual figures who have left their mark on world history—a mark that she clearly has already made for herself even at this point in her career.

Henry M. Christman

part 1
INDIA: THE NATION

§ INAUGURAL ADDRESS TO THE NATION

Broadcast over All India Radio
[New Delhi, January 26, 1966]

Thirty-six years ago, on this very day, my voice was one of thousands repeating the historic and soul-stirring words of our Pledge of Independence.

In 1947 that pledge was fulfilled. The world acknowledged that a new progressive force, based on democracy and secularism, had emerged. In the seventeen years that Jawaharlal Nehru was Prime Minister, the unity of this country with its diversity of religion, community and language became a reality, and democracy was born and grew roots. We took the first step towards securing a better life for our people by planned economic development. India's voice was always raised in the cause of the liberation of oppressed peoples, bringing hope and courage to many. It was heard beyond her frontiers as the voice of peace and reason promoting friendship and harmony among nations.

During his brief but memorable stewardship, Shastriji enriched the Indian tradition in his own way. He has left our country united and determined to pursue our national objectives. Only yesterday we committed his mortal remains to the sacred rivers. The entire country sorrowed for the great loss. I feel his absence intensely and personally, for I worked closely with him for many years.

My own approach to the vast problems which confront us is one of humility. However, the tradition left by Gandhiji and my father, and my own unbounded faith in the people of India give me strength and confidence. Time and again, India has given evidence of an indomitable spirit. In recent years, as in the past, she has shown unmistakable courage and capacity for meeting new challenges. There is a firm base of Indianness which will withstand any trial.

The coming months bristle with difficulties. We have innumerable problems requiring urgent action. The rains have failed us, causing drought in many parts. As a result, agricultural production, which is still precariously dependent on weather and rainfall, has suffered a sharp decline. Economic aid from abroad and earnings from export have not come to us in the measure expected. The lack of foreign exchange has hurt industrial production. Let us not be dismayed or discouraged by these unforeseen difficulties. Let us face them boldly. Let us learn from our mistakes and resolve not to let them recur. I hope to talk to you from time to time to explain the measures we take and to seek your support for them.

Above all else we must ensure food to our people in this year of scarcity. This is the first duty of Government. We shall give urgent attention to the management and equitable distribution of food grains, both imported and procured at home. We expect full cooperation from State Governments and all sections of the people in implementing our plans for rationing, procurement and distribution. Areas like Kerala which are experiencing acute shortage will receive particular attention. We shall try especially to meet the nutritional needs of mothers and children in the scarcity-affected areas to prevent permanent damage to their health. We cannot afford to take risks where basic food is concerned. We propose, therefore, to import large enough quantities of food grains to bridge this gap. We are grateful to the United States for her sympathetic understanding and prompt help.

Only greater production will solve our food problem. We have now a well-thought-out plan to reach water and chemical fertilizers and new high-yielding varieties of seed as well as technical advice and credit to farmers. Nowhere is self-reliance more urgent than in agriculture, and it means higher production not only for meeting the domestic needs of a large and increasing population, but also for growing more for exports. We have to devise more dynamic ways of drawing upon the time and energy of our rural people and engaging them in the tasks of construction. We must breathe new life into the rural works program and see that the income of the rural laborer is increased.

Our strategy of economic advance assigns a prominent role in the public sector to the rapid expansion of basic industries, power and transport. In our circumstances, this is not only desirable but necessary. It also imposes an obligation to initiate, construct and manage public sector enterprises efficiently and to produce sufficient profits for further investments. Within the framework of our plans, there is no conflict between the public and private sectors. In our mixed economy, private enterprise has flourished and has received help and support from Government. We shall continue to encourage and assist it.

Recent events have compelled us to explore the fullest possibilities of technological self-reliance. How to replace, from domestic sources, the materials we import, the engineering services we purchase, and the know-how we acquire from abroad? Our progress is linked with our ability to invent, improvise, adopt and conserve. We have a reservoir of talented scientists, engineers and technicians. We must make better use of them. Given the opportunity, our scientists and engineers have demonstrated their capacity to achieve outstanding results. Take the shining example of Dr. Homi Bhabha and the achievements of the Atomic Energy Establishment. The path shown by Dr. Bhabha will remain an inspiration.

Our program of economic and social development are encompassed in our Plans. The Third Five Year Plan is drawing to a close. We are on the threshold of the Fourth. The size and content of the Fourth Plan received general endorsement of the National Development Council last September even while we were preoccupied with the defense of our country. Its detailed formulation was interrupted due to many uncertainties, including that of foreign aid. We propose now to expedite this work. In the meantime an annual plan has been drawn up for 1966–67, the first year of the Fourth Plan. This takes into account the main elements of the Five Year Plan.

In economic development, as in other fields of national activity, there is a disconcerting gap between intention and action. To bridge this gap, we should boldly adopt whatever far-reaching changes in administration may be found necessary. We must introduce new organizational patterns and modern tools and techniques of management and administration. We shall instill into governmental machinery greater efficiency and a sense of urgency and make it more responsive to the needs of the people.

In keeping with our heritage, we have followed a policy of peace and friendship with all nations, yet reserved to ourselves the right to independent opinion. The principles which have guided our foreign policy are in keeping with the best traditions of our country, and are wholly consistent with our national interest, honor and dignity. They continue to remain valid. During my travels abroad, I have had the privilege of meeting leaders in government and outside and have always found friendship and an appreciation of our stand. The fundamental principles laid down by my father, to which he and Shastriji dedicated their lives, will continue to guide us. It will be my sincere endeavor to work for the strengthening of peace and international cooperation, so that people in all lands live in equality, free from domination and fear. We seek to maintain the friendliest relations with our neighbors and to resolve any disputes peacefully. The Tashkent Declaration is an expression of these sentiments. We shall fully implement it in letter and spirit.

Peace is our aim, but I am keenly aware of the responsibility of Government to preserve the freedom and territorial integrity of the country. We must, therefore, be alert and keep constant vigil, strengthening our defenses as necessary. The valor, the determination, the courage and sacrifice of our fighting forces have set a magnificent example. My thoughts go out today to the disabled and the families of those who gave their lives.

Peace we want because there is another war to fight—the war against poverty, disease and ignorance. We have promises to keep with our people—of work, food, clothing and shelter, health and education. The weaker and underprivileged sections of our people—all those who require special measures of social security—have always been and will remain uppermost in my mind.

Youth must have greater opportunity. The young people of India must recognize that they will get from their country tomorrow what they give her today. The nation expects them to aspire and to excel. The worlds of science and art, of thought and action beckon to them. There are new frontiers to cross, new horizons to reach and new goals to achieve.

No matter what our religion, language or State, we are one nation and one people. Let us all—farmers and workers, teachers and students, scientists and technologists, industrialists, businessmen, politicians and public servants—put forth our best effort. Let us be strong, tolerant and disciplined, for tolerance and discipline are the very foundations of democracy. The dynamic and progressive society, the just social order which we wish to create, can be achieved only with unity of purpose and through hard work and cooperation.

Today I pledge myself anew to the ideals of the builders of our nation—to democracy and secularism, to planned economic and social advance, to peace and friendship among nations.

Citizens of India, let us revive our faith in the future. Let us affirm our ability to shape our destiny. We are comrades in a mighty adventure. Let us be worthy of it and of our great country. *Jai Hind* (Victory to India).

§ FOOD

**From address to State Chief Ministers
and Agriculture Ministers**
[New Delhi, April 9, 1966]

I consider this conference to be one of very great importance. It would be no exaggeration to say that if we take the right decisions here and follow them up with prompt and concrete action, we should have determined the pattern of national life for some years to come.

I am glad to be able to meet you so soon after my visit to the world capitals. I am happy that, as a result of this visit, there is greater sympathy for our country and greater appreciation of our economic and international policies. There have been renewed assurances of more food aid and more assistance for our development plans. The outlook for our Fourth Plan has definitely improved and that is indeed a big gain.

All over the world, there is considerable concern at our food shortage. Although for years we have been importing food to meet deficits, this year's drought came as a tremendous reminder to the advanced nations of the troubles of the developing world. There has been warm response from all parts of the globe. The speedy passage which the new food bill had in the United States Congress is proof of this new awareness.

We are most grateful for all this sympathy and help. But let me remind you that friends will help only if they are convinced that we are doing our best to help ourselves. Unless we increase agricultural production rapidly, control our population, and thus achieve self-sufficiency in the next few years, we will have forfeited our right to call ourselves a free country, let alone a great country. We must become self-reliant. Aid and help should be a temporary phase.

I am confident that we are well set on the way to self-reliance. Last year's reverse on the food front should not blind us to the gains made under the three Five Year Plans. Even in regard to agriculture, we recorded a 70-percent increase in fifteen years. But what is more important is that we are on the threshold of much larger increases. In the first phase, the increase came to us mainly through traditional methods like bringing more areas under cultivation and irrigation. We have at last moved on to a higher level of agricultural technology. The High-yielding Varieties Program, the Intensive Agricultural Development Program and the Intensive Agricultural Areas Program represent this second phase. They rest on the use of heavier doses of fertilizer, the choice of new seeds which promise a breakthrough in production, and the adoption of plant protection measures. All these should be managed by a truly modern agricultural administration.

Consumption of fertilizers has been increasing rapidly. In 1965–66, the figure stood at 6 lakh tons in terms of nitrogen. Next year, it will be 10 lakh tons. In 1965–66, we spent Rs. 1.3 crore on pesticides; next year, we will spend Rs. 22 crore. The outlay for short-term credit will go up from Rs. 375 crore to 450 crore. We shall also spend an additional Rs. 40 crore on rural electrification. Then, there is this scientific program of bringing land under the high-yielding varieties. Nearly five million acres are to be brought under such varieties of seed in 1966–67. In the Fourth Plan period, we hope that a total of 32.5 million acres will come under such seeds.

We have already gathered some momentum; this must be kept up. There can be no more slackness. There is only one direction in which we can go, and that is forward. We cannot afford another crop failure.

While we must be firm on the essentials, we should be flexible and ready to try out new approaches in the interest of the ultimate goal. From this point of view, I commend the decision to increase the target area for plant protection. It is only right to raise the target, for there are exaggerated stories of grain being wasted or consumed by rodents and insects. But merely to raise the target is not enough. To allocate more foreign exchange for import of pesticides is not enough. How soon will a trained staff be available with the right tools and supplies? What matters is not what we say but how we organize our business.

Another area where flexibility is called for is agricultural credit. We have been stressing the importance of channeling credit through cooperatives. But if cooperatives cannot do it fast enough, they have to be supplemented. The Government has an inescapable responsibility for meeting the farmers' requirements. The cultivator must be able to get adequate credit and at the right time.

Another welcome departure is the experiment being tried out in Andhra Pradesh, under which the farmer is offered credit in the form of inputs in return for which he agrees to give the Government agencies an equivalent quantity of grain. This kind of repayment in kind has worked well in Japan and Taiwan. In our country, too, it is an old idea which can be applied in the new conditions. Our Food Corporation is authorized by its charter to make advances in return for an agreement to deliver grain. This effectively links credit and marketing.

I now turn to the subject of organization and allocation of responsibility. In earlier years, whenever the subject of agricultural administration was discussed, almost always the first suggestion was to have an all-India agricultural service with more security. Perhaps this constant search for personal security has been at the root of most of our ills. It is more important to give recognition to quick and good work than to give security to those who fail. How else can we improve methods and performance? I am glad to find in the agenda papers that it is now proposed to place responsibility for agricultural production squarely on the shoulders of specified officials—the agricultural production officer at the district level and the commissioner at the State level. It is not enough to draw up right schemes for doing away with confusion and divided responsibility. Three or four months from now, we must examine how many States have actually enforced such unified lines of command.

If a person is answerable for his deeds or lapses, he must know the area of his responsibility. This applies to governments also. It is, therefore, a good idea to have some clear understanding between the State Governments and the Union Government as to who does what. Take the high-yielding seed varities. Who will supply them? Who will grow them, grade them, store them, distribute them? In the same way, who will find the fertilizer needed by intensive programs? Clear prior understanding will cut down needless paper chasing and the journeying back and forth from Delhi.

Various governments and private organizations all over the world are sending us large quantities of milk powder, vitamin tablets, baby food, and so forth. These generous gifts are meant for children, pregnant and nursing mothers, the aged and the disabled. The utmost vigilance should be exercised to ensure that these gifts reach the people for whom they are meant. We should give no occasion for any complaint in their distribution.

We often say that we have accorded agriculture the topmost priority. This is only stating the obvious. Without a marked advance in agriculture, there is no future for the country. Agriculture is a matter not only of financial allocation but also of efficient administration. What is required is to convey the right kind of inputs to the right place at the right time. To this task must be bent all the energies of the State Governments and the Union Government.

From address to State Chief Ministers
[New Delhi, September 26, 1967]

I do not think one can overestimate the importance of solving
our food problem. In my view, our honor is involved here, our security is involved, the lives of our people are involved. It is true
that we may not be able to find any positive solutions this year. It
may take a little more time. But whatever we do, it should be part
and parcel of an integrated thinking The note which has been
circulated says that any policy, however sound and logical, will fail
to achieve this objective if all States do not unreservedly accept the
assumption underlying it and fully discharge their commitment.
The Food Minister, I am sure, will go into the details. His Ministry has already circulated a report and we have statistics of one
sort or another. The Food Corporation has been having intensive
and extensive consultations with all the State Governments. All
these should lead to a common acceptance of certain fundamental
principles.

Can we not at least jointly say that we shall do whatever lies in
our power never again to let the country or even parts of it pass
through the kind of crisis with which we have been faced during
the last two years or so? It is important to have this resolve, but it
is equally important that it is translated into practice, village by
village, *tahsil* by *tahsil,* district by district and State by State.

This year, we anticipate a good harvest, but we should not be
complacent. A good harvest will be of no use unless those who
produce it get a reasonable return on their labor and investment. It
will be of no use unless we build up a buffer stock against future
hazards of rain or lack of rain. We must procure sufficient quantities of food grains. Internally, we must ensure that the prices are
kept stable so that antisocial elements, hoarders and profiteers can
have no hope of making money from the misery and starvation of
our people.

All efforts should be made to maximize procurement both for
the State and for the Central buffer stock from within our own
production. We recognize that the pipeline has dried up. We recognize that there are no reserves and, therefore, we have to import.
We shall try to do so. But we must also be firm in our resolve to

keep imports to the very minimum. All this will have to be done in terms of practical considerations and taking into account the existing situation. It is essential to mobilize all our efforts and resources to begin procurement from the very commencement of the *kharif* season. The Agricultural Prices Commission has provided us the structure of procurement prices. I am sure you will discuss this and reach a quick decision. Quite clearly, procurement is required not merely for buffer stocks, but also for the public distribution system. Such a system needs to be maintained in order to ensure price stabilization throughout the year. Government is determined to achieve this end.

If one looks at the problems of our country in the light of reason and rationality, one is bound to recognize the fact that there can be no salvation for any one part of India unless there is salvation for the country as a whole.

Looking at each State in isolation is fraught with dangerous consequences not only for that particular State but for all of us. So I earnestly hope that, throughout these deliberations, the Chief Ministers, regardless of their political predilections, will consider the problems not only from the point of view of the interests of their States, but also from the national point of view.

I must thank the Chief Ministers of the surplus States for the help they have given. Some of them could no doubt have helped a little more, and I hope that our able Food Minister will be able to persuade them to do so. We at the Center are conscious of the difficulties which each one of you faces in your particular State, and we do not want to minimize those difficulties. But if the nation as a whole suffers, those difficulties will also increase a hundredfold. So, I would once again stress the point that we should make an attempt here to look at the larger problem of India as a whole and see how we can solve it both in the short-term and the longer-term aspects.

§ THE PUBLIC SECTOR

Address inaugurating round-table discussion
[New Delhi, June 14, 1966]

There is no such thing as "public sector technology" or "private sector technology." It is the same with project planning, costing, research, marketing and the rest. The public sector must stand or fall, like the private sector, on the tests of efficiency, profit, service and technological advance. The only difference lies in the fact of social control and social purpose with regard to the public sector. The "philosophy" might be different. The operation is similar.

We advocate a public sector for three reasons: to gain control of the commanding heights of the economy; to promote critical development in terms of social gain or strategic value rather than primarily on considerations of profit; and to provide commercial surpluses with which to finance further economic development.

The public sector in India today is a large and growing family. We have industrial units such as Hindustan Steel; construction units like the National Projects Construction Corporation; design and engineering units like the National Industrial Development Corporation and Engineers (India) Ltd.; financial units like the State Bank and the Life Insurance Corporation; trading units like the State Trading Corporation; and service units like the Shipping Corporation and Export Credit Guarantee Corporation. We also have railways, post and telegraph departments, ordnance factories, river valley projects, commodity boards and national laboratories. The State Governments have their own public sector undertakings like electricity boards and State transport undertakings. Together, all these constitute a large and critical aggregate of investment spread over a wide field.

The public sector, however, can claim no virtue unless it functions effectively as an instrument of production and development and as a creator of new wealth. Here, the results have, on the whole, fallen below our expectations. Some undertakings have done extremely well; others have fared poorly. Many are making indifferent progress. This is a matter for national concern. I certainly am anxious to see that impediments in the way of the smooth and efficient working of the public sector are removed. We should consider this question in three or four parts. First comes the stage of project planning, and then the stage of construction, erection and starting up. These two stages constitute the gestation period. The third stage is reached with the commissioning of the unit. This is the stage of operation. This also includes sales and exports. The last stage is the stage of expansion, diversification and technological refinement. This includes research and development and the acquisition of design capability.

Many of the difficulties of the public sector belong to the gestation period itself. Faulty planning with regard to concept, size, location, raw materials, design, choice of processes, equipment, personnel, contractual arrangements, supervision, coordination, time schedules, and so forth, has resulted in cost escalation and delay. Overcapitalization, overstaffing, incidentally adding to township costs, inadequate work-study, lack of delegation of power, the application of secretarial codes and procedures to commercial undertakings, faulty system of financial control and audit, and the lack of a well-thought-out personnel policy, constitute another set of problems. The proper programming of orders, pricing policies, quality and cost controls, research and design development and the structure of management are other factors which need looking into. Labor relations have not always been satisfactory.

My purpose is not to list all the problems, but to suggest the need for a close, hard look at every aspect of the public sector. There has yet to be a satisfactory reconciliation between autonomy and accountability. Some of these problems are no more than teething troubles, while others are products of inexperience. We must learn from our mistakes.

The public sector, too, must set an example in self-reliance. We should not have to go in for turnkey jobs or foreign collaboration the second or third time. Our engineers, scientists and technicians are second to none. Government has been too cautious and conservative in giving them greater opportunity to show their worth.

There can be no stereotype for the public sector. It must grow, evolve and change with the times. In another twenty years, the public sector might well be larger than the Government in terms of personnel and budget. A new generation of industrial and scientific civil servants will have come into being. We have to plan for that day.

It would also be useful to study the working of the public sectors in other countries. Italy, for example, has a large and flourishing public sector which is highly competitive and often works in partnership with private enterprise. Also, it has embarked on an ambitious program for developing southern Italy, which is the less developed half of that country. Sweden offers another pattern of public enterprise and initiative. In France, large successful corporations like Renault and Sud Aviation are state-owned. In Germany, Volkswagen has been developed in the public sector. We should keep all these examples and developments in mind and never shut our eyes to the possibility of improvement and change.

As I said, the final test lies in profitability, service and growth If the public sector cannot pass these tests, then there is no meaning in it. I am confident that the public sector in India is quite capable of delivering the goods, provided it is allowed to function.

This is an informal gathering, and I hope you will speak frankly and carry forward the debate on this important topic in a manner that will assist us in ensuring that the public sector truly becomes a creator of new wealth.

§ ECONOMIC PLANNING

Address to the National Development Council
[New Delhi, December 1, 1967]

It is time for us to affirm our will and determination to boldly seek a solution of our basic problems through planned effort, relying more and more on our own resources of men and material to forge and sustain a satisfactory pace of progress.

As those on whom is cast the great responsibility of guiding the affairs of the country at this stage, we have to realize that to bring about ordered progress in the country, we cannot yield to the temptation of enjoying transient popularity either with the masses or with organized vested interests, of surrendering to shortsighted views in matters of vital importance concerning our development. Such surrender would only cause delay and place difficulties in the way of our self-reliant progress. Spontaneous support, whether by way of acceptance of certain tasks and obligations or sacrifice of narrow self-interest, will not be forthcoming for the measures which may be necessary without sufficient education and understanding of the very complex issues involved. Unfortunately, we hesitate to explain to the people frankly and frequently enough what the situation is, or to tell them the pros and cons of our proposals, or to provide them clear guidance as to what they should do in a given situation. Or, it may be that, not fully confident of our capacity to carry the people with us, we resort to policies and programs which are halting and compromising and wholly inadequate to meet our problems satisfactorily and to create conditions of popular understanding and enthusiasm.

It is only in a spirit of resolute purpose and confidence in our people that we should set out on our next phase of planned development, which has to be a phase of accelerated and self-reliant progress.

The time now is for clear thinking and decisiveness. After two years of catastrophic mishaps, mainly due to severe droughts and wars whose costs yet remain uncalculated, we are in a hopeful situation with regard to agricultural production. Prosperity in the rural areas will make an impact on the rest of the economy. If we are able to pursue right policies, on the basis of the potential already built up in the economy, it should be possible in the next year to achieve a further increase in the national income. Thus, in two years we could nearly resume the interrupted rate of growth and provide a convincing demonstration of the resilience of our economy. If a high rate of growth can be later sustained as a normal rate of growth by the bold steps taken in the interim period, we would have converted a setback into a real and permanent advance. During the next year, our principal task should be to extract the maximum out of the productive capabilities which have been built in agriculture and in industry.

We shall have to take measures to restore the rate of capital formation, as quickly as possible, to at least the levels which were reached two years ago. An increase in the rate of capital formation, progressively supported by a larger proportion of domestic savings, is at the core of the process of dynamic development. In the last two bad years, we have lost ground in this regard. But this can be and must be recovered by purposeful action in the next one or two years.

Then there is the problem of a large deficit in our international trade. Our imports are more than a thousand million dollars in excess of our exports. In the present international climate of aid and in pursuance of our policy of achieving early self-reliance, we must seek to reduce this gap quickly and ultimately eliminate it by following a vigorous policy of export promotion and import substitution, and keeping rational economic calculations in mind so that the nation takes the maximum advantage of its resources. As a substantial part of this deficit arises because of our dependence on the imports of food grains, fertilizers, oil, metals and machinery, we must concentrate on the development of their production in the right proportion, taking into account the increasing needs of the future. Exports must rise and every reasonable support required for this purpose should be provided to bring the day of self-reliance nearer. In fact it is with this that our strategy of development has been concerned, and for which it has been striving over the last ten years with different degrees of success. The constant unthinking criticism of our Plans and policies has served to confuse the issues. I think that our efforts are now bearing fruit. We can look forward to a growing, dynamic agriculture. We are increasingly able to support a program of increased capital formation on the basis of our own resources. In fact the situation at the moment is rather anomalous. We have idle capacity in the capital goods sector where only a few years ago we had to depend largely on imports. This situation has arisen not because we have suddenly become a great steel-producing and machine-building nation. It has happened mainly because of the lower rate of capital formation which was forced upon us during the last two years. The remedy for this situation is to get back to the required rate of capital formation as quickly as possible, so that the gap between the capacities created and the production required is eliminated.

The problem is how to mobilize financial resources to enable us to make a fuller use of our capacities. It seems that during the next one or two years we are not likely to be short of the real resources required for increased investment, such as steel, cement and machinery of various kinds. But some arrangement has to be found to finance the necessary outlays without accentuating inflationary pressures.

Also, it is clear that if the public sector expenditure on development is to be expanded, we shall have to pay for developmental outlays for the purchase of materials, for payment of labor, and so forth. The obligation to meet this expenditure has to be assumed by the community. Ultimately this must be reflected in higher savings and taxation. Logically, there should be no problem so long as the share comes out of a substantial rise in national income, which is the object and result of development. In a democratic system this task is not an easy one. The issue is simple. To develop the country, the Government, both at the Center and in the States, must have sources of revenue, but if people, even those who greatly benefit from development, are not willing to pay taxes, what is the way out? Is our effort adequate for our development? The savings of the community, which represent the "effort" put into development and are a token of our concern for the future advance, are very low. Should capital formation be supported entirely by such poor domestic savings?

In the long run we should barely expect to keep our per capita income from falling below its current level, especially if the population continues to grow at 2.5 percent. Thus, it is absolutely necessary to give very serious attention to the issues which are of crucial importance to development. Our sincerity about following a course of self-reliant growth will be tested by our attention to these issues.

Resources are not calculated in terms of money alone, but also in extracting the maximum out of the potentialities of the economy. Once we begin to contract, resources will become smaller and smaller and our situation will become much worse. This will be neither planning nor progress but merely sliding down. A slowing down in capital formation will, however, be justified if it is clearly designed (1) to bring the economy into balance; (2) to provide for reducing the vulnerability of uncertain factors by organizing buffer stocks; and so forth; (3) to adjust prices so as to provide the right basis for future economic calculations and the mobilization of future resources; (4) to make the adjustment for better utilization of capacity; and (5) to generally restore financial stability. In short, it could mean taking one step backward to enable one to take two steps forward later on.

The process of development is a continuous one. The boundaries between the Plans and the length of Plan periods are arbitrary. As long as the effort is not weakened and the absence of a formal Plan is not used as an excuse for slackening the effort, any controversy regarding the dates and periods of planning is not terribly important.

I welcome you all once more. We attach great value to your opinions and to the experience which you have had in your respective States. I sincerely hope that sitting here and debating these matters together we can have fruitful discussions and evolve a path which will take us all forward.

From address to the National Development Council
[New Delhi, May 17, 1968]

The National Development Council is charged with the responsibility of providing guidelines to the Planning Commission. The detailed work on planning can be undertaken only when you have given the indications. I should like to emphasize at this stage that we are not concerned with the details of the Plan in this meeting but only with the basic approach to the Plan. Of course, this is just as important because it circumscribes the Plan itself to some extent. The major issues are the overall goals which we seek, the tempo and pattern of development, the national effort, discipline, cooperation and determination required for reaching the set goals. We have, for instance, to address ourselves to the problem of the rate of growth. Do we consider it adequate or do we think that it should be less or more? If we think that a rate of 5 percent or 6 percent is essential, are we prepared to make the necessary effort in terms of mobilization of resources?

Despite the progress registered in many directions, the broad fact remains that the real income per head is exceedingly low. Growth has not made a significant impact on the living standards of the people, and has not provided opportunities for full employment or for reducing disparities. That is why the rate of growth in the future is a matter of crucial importance. Planning for a 6-percent growth of the economy in conditions of diminishing external aid is a bold undertaking. Are we prepared to undertake it? Is there the national will for this? On the other hand, can we possibly do less? Our efforts necessarily must be strenuous. We need, therefore, a firm direction, a longer perspective and commitment to action.

The National Development Council is the supreme body of our nation and can give this lead and impart this confidence to our people. The right policies and programs must be backed by the necessary resources, physical as well as financial. If we aim at having a buffer stock of food grains, it has to be financed as part of the program of price stability. Agricultural development must be promoted and credit facilities extended increasingly to the weaker sections of the agriculturists. The infrastructure of irrigation, fuel, power, roads, transport and communications will have to be expanded. Basic industries will also have to be expanded, especially to promote rapid industrialization on a broad basis. Many programs will have to be undertaken in the field of education, health, scientific research, technological development, and for the promotion of engineering design and consultancy services. We will have to devise methods to enlarge our resources, in particular the governmental revenues which would enable the Governments at the Center and in the States to discharge their responsibilities.

I am sure the members of the council will give serious thought to this problem of resource mobilization. We cannot talk of progressive elimination of PL-480 grain imports and the reduction of foreign aid without devising the ways and means to raise the necessary additional resources. A large part of the annual increases in income will accrue in the rural sector, particularly amongst the prosperous farmers who will benefit by the developmental effort. It is evident that the mobilization of resources must take full cognizance of this fact. Our attitude in this matter should cease to be equivocal.

Another range of problems to which the Planning Commission has drawn attention is related to the operation of a mixed economy. A number of questions arise. What combination of market forces and administrative directions is most suitable for resource allocation? What role should be assigned to the public sector, and how can it be made important and effective? How do we encourage private enterprise without concentration of wealth and economic power? The Planning Commission has tried to strike a balance between the various sectors and has made proposals for consideration. In this respect, again, we must provide a clear lead and guidance.

I hope the Chief Ministers will pardon me if I mention a problem which has been worrying me. There is sometimes talk of fighting the Center. I cannot see how the country can be strengthened by any such infighting, or by the tensions which it is bound to generate. The present situation requires a concerted and united effort to pull out of the rut in which we find ourselves. I want to assure the Chief Ministers that I am fully aware of the difficulties which confront our States and sympathize with their just demands. I am unhappy that we cannot do all that is needed to help them. But I do hope that in this meeting we shall not follow the old pattern of reiterating our grievances against the Center or against anyone else, but will make a conscious effort to assess the major economic difficulties on a national plane and see how each State can play its part to overcome them. Only thus can a situation be created when the Center will be in a position to come to the assistance of the States.

I am told that even without planning we could achieve some growth. But it is obvious that this kind of growth would give rise to acute tensions in society. A free market economy can bring economic growth but will not bring the kind of equality of opportunity which the vast masses of our underprivileged expect. We are pledged to look after the needs of the weaker sections of the community and the backward areas of the country. Surely the aim of planning was not only to budget our resources but to find ways to advance faster so that increasing population and growing needs do not outstrip our national advance. Surely planning was also to be an instrument for correcting imbalances and lessening disparities.

I think I have indicated some of the issues which are before us. I shall now request the Deputy Chairman of the Planning Commission to explain in greater detail some of the underlying assumptions and problems inherent in the approach to the Fourth Five Year Plan.

§ COOPERATIVES

From Inaugural Address at
the Fifth Indian Cooperative Congress
[New Delhi, December 2, 1967]

In our strategy of development, we want growth and greater equality. We want to prevent concentration of economic power. That is why we must help the public sector as well as the cooperative sector to grow, both absolutely and in relation to the private sector. Cooperatives combine the good points of both the public sector and the private sector. They give a voice and sense of participation to the ordinary man. They are based on voluntary union and democratic control. At the same time, they can take full advantage of modern large-scale management.

If I may say so, the cooperative way is a civilized way of working, providing as it does the means of diminishing large-scale ownership by individuals and groups, but without sacrificing the advantages of big units essential for the application of modern science and technology. The cooperative thus bridges the gap between the small unit and technology. Dreams cannot become realities, unless there are material factors by which we can implement them. It is only through science and technology that we can supply these material conditions.

Even the so-called advanced countries assign a major role to cooperatives. Therefore, I feel, they fulfill a more extensive economic function than we are normally aware of. In most European countries as well as in the United States, cooperation is the ruling principle of agriculture. In Japan, cooperatives are a big force.

Whether it is agriculture or industry or the services, cooperatives have made spectacular progress since 1950-51 when we took up planning. I find that the total agricultural credit dispensed by cooperatives was only Rs. 290 million in that year, while last year, the figure rose to Rs. 3450 million. Over the same period, the working capital of all cooperatives has grown nearly nine times. I am particularly impressed by the great strides made by this movement in agricultural processing and marketing sectors. Cooperation is an ideal instrument for rural development. In the Government of India, cooperation is part of the same Ministry which looks after agriculture, community development and food.

But cooperation has as vital a role in urban areas as in rural areas. All over the world, urbanization has led to the erosion of people's ability to live a well-adjusted corporate life. People might reside together in cities but they are isolated and lonely and do not seem to live together. The faster a city grows the less mutual regard and sympathy there seem to be among its people. Cooperation has the capacity to shape groups into communities with shared interests.

Our cooperators should devote more attention to the consumer movement. The utility of consumer cooperatives is not limited to the fight against rising prices. We have another fight, hardly less important, which is that for quality. Cooperatives can ensure quality in what is produced much better than private trade can.

We need much greater participation by cooperatives in banking. In our country, banking has largely remained the preserve of the affluent, at any rate of the middle class and above, not only in its control, but even in its reach. It has cared more for the big man than the small man. Only rarely do we find the common people having recourse to banks. Lately, agricultural cooperatives in some areas have begun advancing credit against an approved production program instead of the security of land.

A well-run cooperative banking program can finance a large number of small entrepreneurs, such as graduates who want to set up small industries, and so forth. Cooperative banks can also attract small savings, especially if they go to the people instead of expecting them to come to them, waiting long hours and filling forms. I believe some banks in western and southern India have already made a beginning on these lines.

Having spoken on the cooperatives, I must also sound a note of caution. Not all that we hear about the actual working of cooperatives is flattering. There is the general belief, which I mentioned, that the cooperatives help the bigger people rather than the small people. Such a state of affairs would defeat the very purpose of the Cooperative Movement. Secondly, our cooperatives seem to have become far too dependent on financial aid from the Government. This is a negation of the basis of cooperation which is self-help and self-reliance. Thirdly, there is also a widely prevalent feeling that cooperatives are too mixed up with politics. I find that you are discussing how to deofficialize the movement. I wish you would also discuss how to depoliticalize it.

The history of the Cooperative Movement in India of the last sixty years shows that wherever the movement is strong, it is due to the selfless work of dedicated individuals who have steadily resisted the temptation of politics. They have regarded cooperation as an alternative form of serving the people. There is great need in the country today, in every walk of life, for selfless people. It is more so in the Cooperative Movement.

Cooperation enshrines the principle that the social good is supreme. It is because cooperation is a form of social control and also helps the common man that my Government is committed to promoting the cooperative sector. We want this sector to become more powerful. At the same time, it should develop internal strength and safeguards, simplify its procedures, and widen its base by increasing its membership. It must not allow a handful of people to dominate its decisions.

§ COMMUNALISM

Address in Parliament
[New Delhi, December 22, 1967]

Communal incidents,[1] which in recent months have marred our national life in certain parts of the country, have caused deep distress as well as anxiety to this House, and to all right-thinking people in the country.

Secularism and democracy are the twin pillars of our State, the very foundations of our society. From time immemorial, the vast majority of our people are wedded to concepts of secularism, religious tolerance, peace and humanity. It is understandable that they should feel outraged and deeply disturbed at the aberrations which appear here and there and afflict small sections of society, and which arouse or exploit communal passions or promote disharmony, tension and violence. It is a matter for satisfaction that even in areas where trouble has occurred, the general public at large, whether belonging to one community or another, has lived in a state of complete harmony and peace. Indeed, there have been many instances in which people of one community have saved the lives and property of their fellow citizens of another community.

The incidents which have occurred should, therefore, arouse the indignant disapproval of our people. I am sure this House will deplore and condemn these incidents and join me in conveying its sympathy to those who have been the unfortunate sufferers of such violence and crime at the hands of misguided elements.

As the House is aware, Government have recently appointed a commission to go into these incidents. The object of the commission will be to ascertain the causes which led to them and to recommend measures to prevent recurrence of such disorders in future.

India has the privilege of being the world's largest composite society, and the home of many great and ancient faiths. Communalism is an evil which divides man and fragments society; it

[1] Conflicts between religious groups.

goes against our very genius and cultural heritage. It holds a threat to the unity and integrity of our country which must be our foremost concern.

The citizenship of India is a shared citizenship. Danger to even one single citizen, to whatever community, caste, religion and linguistic group he may belong, is a danger to all of us and, what is worse, it demeans us all. I am sure the House will join me in an appeal to the people of our country to come forward and work for solidarity and common national purpose. Every man, woman and child should be able to tread on Indian earth without fear and with pride of heart in belonging to this great motherland.

§ FAMILY PLANNING

From Inaugural Address at the Sixth All India Conference on Family Planning
[Chandigarh, November 30, 1968]

It is a pleasure to be amongst people who are dedicated missionaries in the cause of the country's future. Smt. Rama Rau and her colleagues do not need to be preached to on the virtues of family planning, for it is their pioneering work which has been largely responsible for the Government and the people of India recognizing the vital connection between family planning and planning for the country's prosperity.

Family planning is an accepted official policy in India. But our program will not succeed if it remains only an official program. There are some developmental plans which can be taken up and completed by a few for the many. There are programs which can be completed by the Government. But family planning is truly a people's program. Its success rests on individual citizens. They have to be approached, persuaded, prompted and helped to practice family planning. The entire official machinery for family planning, whether at the Center or in the States, is meant for this task of persuasion and assistance.

Recently, in agriculture, we have seen that the people's willingness to adopt new methods has overtaken official effort. This might possibly happen in the family planning program also. It should be proved to every village and to every family that a smaller, more compact family makes for better health and greater happiness for the family and hence for more prosperity for the village.

Since we took up family planning programs three or four years ago with the urgency and earnestness they deserve, we have achieved impressive success in terms of numbers. But the success has been limited, as far as I can see, to certain pockets. The most affluent sections of our population and perhaps those groups which are driven by the desire to improve their standard of living—namely, the urban middle class and the skilled industrial workers—are the ones most forthcoming to take advantage of the facilities offered by the Government.

Any new scheme or project, any program which promises improvement in the living standards of the people is usually taken advantage of by those who are already slightly better off. Higher education helps the urban middle class more than the rural working class. The practice of intensive agricultural production is utilized by those who already have the advantage of irrigation rather than those who are dependent on the rain. Even something as uncontroversial as a library helps only the literate and leaves untouched those who cannot read. Thus, many of our development plans often leave the poorest and the weakest where they are, while the slightly better off become stronger. In the process, disparities increase. The official and the voluntary agencies, the latter more than the former, must strengthen their efforts to reach those who are in the greatest need. Official agencies will be in a hurry to fulfill their targets. Nonofficial agencies may be better able to appreciate the human side of the problem.

The theme of your conference is "Family Planning for Hundred Million Couples." We cannot do without targets. But the danger of fixing targets is that in the quest for figures, the desirable is sometimes subordinated to the practicable. A second danger of the target approach is that too little attention is given to the stabilization of gains through follow-up and maintenance checks.

In the advanced nations, family planning and economic development were practically unrelated. Therefore, they could offer us very little guidance. Their society, church and state were all opposed to family planning, and yet the birth rates fell because married couples wanted smaller families. This is true of Protestant-Puritan countries, Catholic countries, as well as socialist countries, all of which frowned on family planning. Yet family planning was practiced in all those countries. The compelling reason was that progress already made prompted them to ask for more progress. Our own country, with its mass poverty, cannot leave this task to individual motivation, because such motivation comes only after a certain level of education or economic betterment has already been reached.

It is because we cannot afford to wait until such consciousness becomes widespread that we in India require well-planned official programs which are implemented with determination. We have several advantages. Unlike the countries of the West, there is no organized religious opposition. Also, the educated person, especially the doctor, enjoys high prestige and his or her judgment carries weight.

The biggest enemy of family planning in India is the lassitude of our people. Even when they are convinced of the benefits of a course of action they make little attempt to exert themselves. Their enthusiasms are often short-lived. The high lapse ratio is a serious problem. This is the reason for our search for a device that has long-lasting effect.

A new danger to the family planning movement has been discernible for some time, and it shows the link which politics has with all other problems of life. There is propaganda to the effect that the family planning program will upset the relative population ratios of the various groups in our country and thus perhaps weaken their political power or bargaining position. This pernicious doctrine may well convince people because of its fallacy. History shows ample proof of the spread and influence of false beliefs. Workers in the field and all those interested in the family planning program must strive to the utmost to combat this sort of propaganda and to allay these imaginary fears. The control of one's family gives greater opportunities for education and medical care and is, therefore, equally important for all groups, minority or otherwise.

Simultaneous progress in programs of intensive agriculture and family planning can give us the chance of conquering rural poverty. The one cannot be thought of as a substitute for the other. In the agricultural program, the combined effort of extension agencies and scientists produced good results. In the family planning program also, the field programs must be strengthened by training workers, by setting up more teams, by better production and distribution of family planning appliances, by a more forceful and imaginative use of mass media to impart information and to create the right social climate.

Equally important is biological research. For the last hundred years or so, medical research has concentrated its energies on combating death and alleviating pain. In the last few decades, science has also turned its attention to improving agricultural production. Science must now concentrate on the mysteries of birth, so that individual families can regulate their size, nations can regulate their population, and this planet can decide how many people it should support and at what levels of happiness. Grotesque pictures are being painted of a world in which by A.D. 2000, which is not too far away from us now, the bulk of the people will be dying of starvation. This is a great challenge to science not only in our own country but all over the world.

§ REGIONALISM

Address in Parliament
[New Delhi, February 20, 1969]

First of all, I would like to congratulate all those who have succeeded in these elections. We would certainly have liked our Congress colleagues to win but we accept the verdict of the electorate. Those who are sitting in this House or in the Assemblies should not feel that we resent their presence. On the contrary, we welcome them and hope they will make valuable contributions to the debates and to the work of this House and the various Assemblies.

I was very unhappy about what Shri Vajpayee said yesterday. He said that I abused his party [Jan Sangh] during the elections. I would like to make it very clear that I did not abuse his party or anybody else. But I spoke very strongly about certain matters— relating not only to his party but to some other parties also— which to my mind are not in the national interest.

In respect of Jan Sangh, I said that we are not against Jan Sangh as such. I did not tell anybody not to vote for Jan Sangh. But I did appeal to the people that they should make all those parties, whose attitudes are not conducive to national peace, harmony and unity, understand that such attitudes must be discarded. I did not speak strongly against any particular party but against what I considered were wrong attitudes, and I certainly spoke very strongly about it.

The main question that was raised by the mover of the motion was with regard to *senas*.[1] When I speak on those matters, I make it a point not to speak against communalism [2] alone but against all those attitudes which promote casteism, regionalism or parochialism and which make one Indian citizen feel that he does not enjoy the same rights as other citizens of India do.

It does not matter where an Indian citizen chooses to live or work. Today he may be living in Delhi, but tomorrow he may want to live in Tamil Nadu, Andhra Pradesh, West Bengal or somewhere else. Every Indian citizen must have that freedom. What has happened recently in Bombay, what has happened between the people of Telengana and Andhra, or what has happened in other parts of India, is certainly most deplorable and absolutely indefensible. I have spoken out very strongly against Shiv Sena [3] and all such *senas* on various occasions and I have absolutely no hesitation in saying here also that such movements do constitute a

[1] Organized militants.
[2] Religious divisions.
[3] A militant right-wing organization in the Bombay region.

very serious threat to the development, progress and unity of the country.

I am very sorry that the name of one of our great and lion-hearted heroes has been associated with such a movement. I had the privilege of having a part of my education in that part of the country where Shivaji operated, that is, in Poona, and most of our excursions were to the sites of some of the old forts which he captured. I have grown up to regard him as a national hero and not as a Maharashtrian hero or as a hero of a particular region. Although I have not in the same way been connected with Sardar Lachit of Assam, he also had a great name in our history. These are people who belong to the nation, and it is very unfortunate that their names should in any way be associated with anything which has to do with any small part or region of the country.

Bombay is one of our great cities. It is a cosmopolitan city. All these big cities have been built by many communities. People from different parts of the country have brought in their money, their industry and their talent. This is how these cities have grown and prospered and any movement which wants to shut off anybody from them will result in bringing these cities down; instead of their rising and growing and adding to the general strength of the country, they will become much narrower in scope.

I would like to make one brief point in passing. In all such debates some Honorable Members have a great deal to say about the police. We sometimes seem to believe as if the police belongs to some other country. Our police may behave well or not, but they are Indians. Most of them are from relatively poor families. They do not come from the top families or from the exploiting classes. We must all help in creating an atmosphere where policemen can have a more positive, broader and more friendly attitude. Much has changed already. There is a constant effort to see that they view their job not only as a law and order matter, but also as an opportunity of helping the people.

All that I am trying to say is that these issues should not be exploited for narrow party loyalties nor used for mutual recrimination or blaming one another. These are, as many Members pointed out, larger national issues and we must all do some heart-searching about them. Unless we raise these matters to a higher level, it will not be possible to solve them. I do not wish to indulge in accusations but I am fully aware that narrow-minded elements of one kind or another do exist amongst all sections of society. No party is free from them. But the Jan Sangh has a point of view about minorities which I do not think is in the interest of the unity of the country. There are still many people in the country who do fall a prey to feelings of communalism, casteism and regionalism. I have not said, either during the elections or in this House or anywhere else, that the Congress Party is perfect. But we have always been making an effort to try and fight these divisive tendencies.

So far as the Government is concerned, it can and does deal with these situations through many methods. I have been in constant touch with the Chief Ministers of Maharashtra and Andhra Pradesh throughout these days, trying to find out what has been happening from day to day and what other measures could be taken. They are doing all they can. I am not saying that all the problems have been solved. Whenever any solution is found, there is always room for creating a feeling or rousing passions among those who do not like that solution. That is why I am asking for the cooperation of all parties.

In the course of the debate it was perhaps natural that a lot should be said about the midterm elections. In a democracy, parties do grow up and do go down also. There is nothing strange about this. Yet, we seem to get very excited every time a seat is lost here or gained there. The non-Congress parties are not used to winning. So, naturally, when they win, there is a great deal of excitement. We also are not used to losing; so, when we lose we also have a good deal of excitement. It is time now that we take democracy in our stride and welcome those who win and sympathize with those who do not win.

We offer full cooperation to all those who have been elected and all the Governments which have come or will come into being in the States; the Government of India will deal fairly with all the States.

The Center does want to cooperate. But cooperation is not so easy when it is unilateral. We expect some cooperation from the State Governments also, specially on matters which have repercussions in other parts of the country. We have to see how we are going to maintain the unity of the country in a situation where there are Governments of entirely different persuasions in different States.

When we speak of unity, we have to see that we transcend our narrow party interests and reject any course which brings our system into contempt or creates the slightest feeling of insecurity in any citizen of India. I am sure that all right-minded people will agree with this.

I know that sometimes people take up a cause which seems to them just. But those who fight for a cause are not always able to control the emotions aroused on its behalf. I am specially unhappy to hear that at many of the places where disturbances have taken place, a large number of children have been gotten involved in it. This does not help any cause, nor is it good for children and other young people who are at a very decisive and impressionable stage of their lives. We must all see how we can keep them out of such disturbances.

When the country was not free, it was different. At that time, all citizens had to get together to free the country. Again, during the fighting on our borders, the entire country got together. But this is not the way to solve problems between one State and another or between Indians living in the same State. It is this kind of violence and disturbances which must be deplored and condemned in the strongest possible terms. I have no hesitation in doing so. I should like to assure Members from all parts of the country—in this we seek the cooperation of all the parties—that it is the Government's endeavor to enable all the Indian nationals to live and work freely in any part of the country. We must work for an India which is one and which is not fragmented, as our great poet Tagore said, by narrow domestic walls, an India in which there are no high or low and privileged or underprivileged.

§ THE PRIVATE SECTOR

Address at the annual session of
the Federation of Indian Chambers of
Commerce and Industry
[New Delhi, March 15, 1969]

It was with some hesitation that I accepted your invitation,
because I wondered whether these meetings were becoming mere
grievance-ventilating sessions. But as I attach importance to cooperation between Government and the business community, I felt
that this would be a renewed opportunity to bring about greater
understanding between us. Through understanding and cooperation, it would be possible for us to have a fruitful dialogue. Otherwise, on occasions like these one tends to speak from a prepared
position on subjects like taxation and controls, inadequacy of return on capital, and slackness of the capital market. Government is
not unaware of these problems and we are always ready to respond
to suggestions which are reasonable and practicable.

Mr. President, I am glad that you have talked about Government and business sharing common objectives. At the same time
you have referred to possible differences in the approach to these
objectives. Perhaps you would like to see obedience to the laws of
market economy in the hope that it would help to produce wealth
and that wealth so produced would ultimately reach down to the
people. This proposition could have been considered at some other
periods of human history, but not today. The world now is qualitatively different from what it was anytime before. India is very
much a part of the world. In fact some of the movements which
exist elsewhere are found in greater intensity in our country. There
is a stirring of consciousness that riches and poverty are not God's
creation but man's. There is a crisis in civilization, a restlessness of
spirit, and a revolt against unimplemented declarations and hypoc-
risy. There is a demand for participation and involvement. Are we
who work in the political field, or you who work in the field of
commerce and industry, capable of responding to this mood of the
people?

The mood is more understandable in a country like ours where the poor outnumber the rich in overwhelming proportion. But the same mood prevails even in countries which boast of affluence and opulence. No system is perfect, but we have to realize that no economic solution can ignore the social or political context. To allow a haphazard growth of productive forces and to wait for the satisfaction of human needs in God's good time is not an answer to the problems which confront us. The first essential in our country today is to provide the elementary needs of our people.

Of the many matters you have referred to specifically, may I pick up one, namely the question of controls? Government's approach to controls is not a doctrinaire one. We do not believe in controls for the sake of controlling. Nor do we accept the view that controls are bad in themselves. We should prefer that those who are concerned with production and distribution should so conduct their business as to obviate or reduce the need for controls. The most effective remedy would be for the industrial units themselves to exercise self-discipline in such matters. But when this does not happen, it becomes necessary to apply controls so as to regulate the use of scarce resources and to protect the consumer. This is particularly so when competitive conditions do not prevail in many sectors of industry.

Our objective is to infuse social purpose at strategic points in decision-making while avoiding cumbersome and unnecessary intervention. I am fully aware that sometimes our methods have been cumbersome. But in the last few years the structure of controls has been considerably simplified. A number of industries have been exempted from the licensing provisions of the Industries Act. Much greater freedom has been given to industry in the matter of adjusting production to changing requirements. Capital issues control has also been greatly simplified. Distribution and price controls have been progressively streamlined and, in fact, removed from a number of commodities. Licensing of imports for priority industries is on the basis of requirement.

The Planning Commission's "Approach to the Fourth Plan" has indicated lines of further progress in this matter and they are spelt out further in the Fourth Five Year Plan. The broad objective is to confine detailed planning to the key sectors. I would call upon industries to devote greater attention to the formulation and revision of targets. In our fast-changing economy, we can secure balanced industrial development only by continuous study of the trends in demand in India as well as abroad and adjustment of our production plans accordingly.

The broad approach to the reform of the industrial licensing system will also be set out in the Plan. The basic and strategic industries, which require significant investment and foreign exchange, must be carefully planned and subjected to licensing. Priority will have to be given to them in the allocation of scarce resources such as foreign exchange. When the foreign exchange needed for equipment or maintenance is marginal, and the interest of the small and village industries is looked after, there may be no need for industrial licensing.

In a society where affluence and power are tiny specks in the vast sea of poverty, it is not unnatural that monopoly should attract strong hostility. Industrial development is regarded by many in our country as an instrument which has benefited only a few. The problem of the concentration of economic power will have to be dealt with *inter alia* by the adoption of suitable policies by our financial institutions. It is reasonable to expect that large industrial groups should raise a substantially larger part of the finance required for projects than is feasible in the case of smaller groups.

Although the rate of growth is important, progress cannot be adjudged by it alone, but more by the composition of the national product and by the nature of the social forces which are generated by development. Governmental decisions and policies are apt to be judged by individuals according to their own preoccupations. Within the same party or organization there are different approaches and evaluation. You have often spoken about the size of the Plan being too large; at the same time you have urged greater public investment in infrastructure as well as in productive industrial activity.

We shall have to deal more vigorously now with the problem of regional disparities. A committee of the National Development Council is looking into this matter. I should like to clarify that we do not think in terms of one State being less developed than another. The approach is in terms of particular regions. Even a State which on the whole is highly developed may contain pockets which are economically backward. The Planning Commission is working out criteria for the selection of less developed regions for special attention.

Mr. President, you have made mention of foreign investment and collaboration. There is no doubt that these will play a useful role in the implementation of the Fourth Plan. There have been complaints that in the past decisions with regard to proposals for foreign investment and collaboration have been unduly delayed. These and other problems relating to foreign investment and collaboration have been discussed in the seminar which the federation recently helped to organize. The procedure for dealing with these cases has now been streamlined. I am sure that delays will be considerably reduced as the potential investors and collaborators now know clearly the kind of industry in which their help is required. The setting up of the Foreign Investment Board will ensure that decisions in Government are taken more speedily.

The import of technology is useful and may even be essential in several sectors, but we have to rely increasingly on our own resources. Industry has sometimes complained that indigenously developed know-how cannot be applied because it has not been carried to the production stage. Our national research institutions are taking steps to remedy this defect. At the same time, industry should not always opt for the easy path of importing established know-how but should make a genuine effort to utilize what is indigenously available. In fact, much development work could take place in our factories, quite apart from the research work which is being done in the national research institutions. Industry should devote a greater quantum of resources to improvement of our own technology.

If we must import technology, we should do so as cheaply as possible. There has been an unnecessary controversy with regard to the centralized purchase of know-how. The Minister of Industrial Development has fully clarified the position and I hope that there are no misgivings on this score now. The point is simple enough; that is, when a number of units are to be set up in an industry simultaneously or within a limited period, the possibilities of saving foreign exchange by unified purchase of know-how should be explored. When it is to the national advantage to purchase know-how on a unified basis, this possibility should not be overlooked.

As regards delays, I find that many captains of industry have spent considerable energy and words in referring to these matters at different forums. But a delay does not take place merely because one does not wish to make a decision or one thinks that one should sleep over it. Sometimes it takes place because many other factors have to be considered. I have referred earlier to the social and political context. There are situations when there may be a very good economic solution but it may involve the country in other long-term difficulties, which may even impinge on the independence of thinking of the country. And these matters are no less important than the mere solving of an economic problem, because if by that solution you create a political problem of long standing, then obviously the solution is not a good one. So some of the delays are due to our anxiety to progress on an enduring basis which would be acceptable to our people. The stability which we seek along with our economic progress is not only the stability of prices, but also the stability of social, political and economic order. And I do hope that all of you present here will subscribe to these objectives.

The continued prosperity of industry is closely interlinked with that of agriculture. It is necessary for industries which use the products of agriculture as raw material to do everything possible to stimulate agricultural productivity. Research work on commercial crops is being intensified. Industry is helping in this but I should like them to further supplement the efforts of Government to take research to the farmer. The time is ripe now to strike out more vigorously to capture markets both for consumer goods and inputs in the rural areas. It may be necessary to evolve completely new techniques of marketing for this purpose.

As you have mentioned, exports of manufactures have shown a striking increase in recent months. In order to secure our goal of self-reliance, we need to place greater emphasis on the exports of these newer products. It is the Government's policy to give high priority to the needs of exports, in matters such as capacity expansion, allocation of imports and scarce materials. We should not allow the revival of domestic demand to interfere with the steady expansion of our export earnings from the newer manufactures. If total exports are to grow at the rate of 7 percent in the Fourth Plan period, the exports of engineering goods, for example, would have to grow at a substantially higher rate of 15 to 20 percent. As exports are small at present in relation to output, an expansion of exports of this magnitude is not difficult to achieve. But the task can be fulfilled only if it is given the highest priority in our national endeavor.

I was glad to hear of the efforts made by your organization to absorb technical personnel facing unemployment. I should like to refer to another group of persons who need the special attention of Government as well as of industry. During the last emergency, a large number of educated young men were commissioned to meet defense needs. Some of them have had to be released from their commissions. The Government is trying to rehabilitate these officers who have all proved their qualities of leadership and capacity for decision. I do hope that private industry will also play its part in utilizing their services. The Directorate General of Resettlement of the Defense Ministry will be glad to provide the information which you might require.

When I spoke from this forum last time, I referred to people who are not directly members of the federation, namely, the wives of members. I had heard that they were doing good social work, and I should like to make a suggestion to them which concerns all of you as well. It is about the employment of people who may be handicapped physically but without interference with their capacity for doing other types of work. A person may not be able to use his legs but he may be a good writer, a good typist, a good accountant. It is necessary to awaken the conscience of society to the plight of these people and see whether we can help them to rehabilitate themselves. This problem has always been with us. But after the fighting on our borders, it has acquired a more acute form, because we have many of our brave soldiers who find themselves in this tragic plight. This might be one direction in which the women who have taken up various aspects of social work could help these handicapped brothers of ours. In many countries, there are actually laws which provide for a small percentage of them to be absorbed. We do not want to go to that extent. But we do hope that this problem will be viewed with sympathy.

I spoke earlier of the contrast between the rich and the poor in our country. This is a situation which is very real and none of us can ignore it or bypass it for a moment. Everything we do is conditioned by our history, by the forces which have made this land what it is today, and by the situation as it exists in our cities and our villages.

The problem is made more acute because we have chosen the democratic system which gives room for ventilating of difficulties, of grievances, of inequalities, and encourages social urges to come to the surface. It also affords opportunity for the exploitation of these grievances if they are not dealt with in time.

I am reminded of the early days of our national movement. The premier national organization was at first content to be a petitioning and a protesting body until Mahatma Gandhi made it a major force for social change and unlocked its inner strength. Several men of great vision belonging to the industrial and business community became identified with the cause of national liberation. As my father used to say, if we work for a great cause, something of the greatness falls on all of us. You have to find an answer to your own satisfaction to the question whether the prestige enjoyed by the present-day captains of industry is equal to the prestige which the great founders of our economic regeneration enjoyed during the period of our national struggle. I should like to see this august body, this federation, become not merely an enlightened forum of discussion for industrialists but a moral force insisting upon the promotion of the highest levels of quality, integrity, public service, national self-reliance, dedication and—the most precious of all things—national self-respect. The economic history of other countries shows us that it is not through governmental edicts and laws that one enforces respect. Respect has to be earned and one has to live in the first as in the last analysis by the applause of one's own people.

I am glad that you have referred to the achievements of the people of our great country in the last few years. We are fully conscious that these achievements are nowhere near sufficient to satisfy our own objectives or the needs of our people. But it is not by decrying ourselves that we can build national self-confidence. This can be done by acknowledging the achievements and by being aware of the deficiencies. As poet Tagore wrote, "If you weep for the sun, you also miss the stars." We have not found a place in the sun yet.

You referred to us as a developed country. Actually while some small areas are developed, many large areas are either undeveloped or developing. And this creates special problems, because we simultaneously have the problems of undeveloped nations as well as the problems of developing nations and of developed nations. I believe in accepting difficulties as a challenge. Only that nation which accepts challenges can grow in strength. No nation has grown to greatness without facing hardships with courage. If we, you and all sections of the Indian people can combine in this endeavor, then shall we be able to face the difficulties, find solutions to our problems, and create a kind of India which is the right of the Indian people to expect.

From Inaugural Address at the annual session of the All India Manufacturers Organization
[New Delhi, May 10, 1969]

In your thoughtful address [1] you have rightly observed that the country's welfare and progress demand close cooperation between Government and entrepreneurs. The understanding of each other's points of view is the starting point of such cooperation. It is in that spirit that I address you today.

The decade which is drawing to a close was to be the "Decade of Development." But our expectations have been belied. In our own country we have been through a number of harrowing experiences in quick succession and this has checked the march of development.

Yet these very setbacks have made planning all the more necessary. The realization is also dawning that the problems generated by the recession, such as the unemployment of the educated, can be solved only by regaining the tempo of development. We must make up for lost time. Our economic problems present a special challenge at this stage of transition to a higher level of technology. This would have been the case even without the invasions on our borders, the drought and the political uncertainties that we have

---

[1] Address by the President of the All India Manufacturers Organization.

been through. You have rightly said that change generates challenge. Our expectations grow; competition grows between class and class and between one region and another. Fortunately, the gradual easing of the agricultural crisis and of the industrial recession has enabled us to move forward decisively and to bring about a new outlook amongst our people.

The Fourth Plan has now been launched. I shall be interested in your comments and criticism. Constructive criticism is always welcome and it is right that the Plan should evoke countrywide discussion. But while the debate is still on, we must implement the Plan.

We find again and again that the mere fulfillment of statistical targets is not enough. Planning is not a game of numbers. It has always been an exercise in social engineering; this is more so today. Our planning must increasingly provide dependable solutions to social problems. Targets themselves represent some of the social objectives. But statistics should not make us lose sight of the social facts behind the figures.

We want a higher growth rate in agriculture and industry, but the price we pay for it should not be in greater disparities and larger concentration of economic power. The Government cannot content itself with the creation of the infrastructure, leaving the building of the superstructure for individuals to do as they like. The State has the responsibility of building a fabric which ensures economic strength combined with social justice. I am glad, therefore, that you have recognized and accepted the directive powers of the State as also the important role played by the public sector in response to economic necessities and in pursuit of the social objectives of our people.

The public sector must justify itself by its efficiency. I agree that a basic requirement for increased efficiency in the public sector is the induction of professional expertise instead of mere administrative talent. We often speak of the constraint of resources. This is real enough, but even more real is the shortage of managerial ability, a shortage shared by public and private sectors alike. It is easier to raise capital, to build buildings and to install machinery than to develop the managerial skills necessary to run a plant at a high degree of efficiency. It is easier to buy technical know-how than to develop it ourselves. It is harder still to unite technical and managerial know-how under the same roof. For tasks which demand initiative, comprehension and competence, we must have the best men, from wherever we can and whatever be their background—whether they are in the public or in the private sector. The shortcomings in the private sector are supposed to recoil only on the entrepreneurs; although this is not wholly true because private enterprise also involves the wealth of the nation. But shortcomings in public sector management directly involve the money and the hopes of the people as a whole.

As a result of numerous studies, we have initiated several steps to improve the performance of the public sector. Our appointments now do reflect a trend towards the employment of more persons with professional understanding and grasp of industry and business.

You have said that resource generation is more important than resource mobilization. Is this not only a partial truth? Unmobilized resources are dead resources, and we need resources even to locate and develop resources. For example, the finding and exploiting of oil reserves or deposits of other minerals demand investment. Water is a resource. Land by itself is a resource. When water is brought to the land, we have a resource mobilized for a purpose. But to bring about this combination, considerable investment is required in irrigation projects. From where can this investment come if not from the mobilization of other resources which have already been created? Only a small portion can come as aid. Hence our whole strategy has been to mobilize, invest and add to our resources, and absorb part of the additional wealth so generated.

Another important point you have raised is about regional imbalances which create social tensions. This is a matter of deep concern to me. There have been agitations in several parts of the country, highlighting the political consequences of economic disparities. Gone are the days when people were resigned to their lot and accepted the affluence of others as a decree of Providence. Each individual wants a place for himself and rightly so. If he sees others get more, his impatience increases. This is true also of regions.

Certain regional imbalances arise out of the uneven distribution of natural endowments. You cannot move a river or a mine from where it is, but you can carry water from the river or move minerals over long distances. A dam or a factory benefits not only the region where it is situated but the country as a whole.

In industrial location technoeconomic considerations must prevail over others. But at the same time, we must do all we can to redress the special backwardness of the less developed regions. The Government's policy, aided by alert public opinion and parliamentary pressure, gives high priority to the development of backward regions. The private sector also can do much. I am glad to say that your organization has commended to industrialists the need to set up industries in areas which have so far been neglected. Government has offered many kinds of rebates and incentives to make up for the absence of infrastructure advantages in such regions, and we are willing to consider any other constructive suggestions in the matter.

In your address, you have also referred to the delay in the creation of a National Power Grid. Your criticism is valid; but an examination of the reasons for the delay will give an inkling of some of the problems of planning, especially when the responsibility is shared. Decisions are sometimes delayed because they must be governed by reasoning, argument and the interplay of regional and national considerations. We are all agreed that there should be a National Grid. We have taken a decision on it. However, the implementation was, to a very large extent, the responsibility of the States. This responsibility is jealously safeguarded by the States. Consequently, many programs of national importance, such as the grid, can be implemented only through the processes of persuasion. We had hoped that the States would build the grid lines on their own, but State Electricity Boards were reluctant to do so. That is why, in the Fourth Plan, we have taken up the grid as a Centrally sponsored scheme. The work will have to be done by the States, but the financial resources will be provided by the Center. At the same time it is worth noting that regional grids have done good work in the north, south and east. Rihand power has helped Calcutta. Mysore power was fed into Tamil Nadu at the time when insufficient rains affected power production there. Sharavati and Koyna have been linked. Tarapur serves both Maharashtra and Gujarat.

It is through the Plan that our economy can move forward and it is for the Plan to set right economic wrongs. The Fourth Plan may not have many new eye-catching projects, but it has addressed itself earnestly to the task of achieving results out of the investments made so far and also of anticipating some of our future needs. Does it matter if there is less fanfare? So long as determination and dedication are there, the objectives of self-sufficiency in food and of reduced reliance on foreign aid are of high importance. We have had too facile a recourse to foreign assistance and collaboration, both financial and technological. If we do not take a second look at collaboration, it can easily become a habit-forming drug. It is incumbent on all who seek to serve our country to give first option to Indian know-how and Indian talent which are now available. Therefore, I commend the Plan to you and seek your wholehearted cooperation in implementing it.

I thank you for your invitation and assure you that we shall always think of you as partners in progress. I hope that the vision and patriotism of your founder will always inspire your organization. I am glad that you are perpetuating his memory by establishing a World Trade Center. This is indeed an imaginative idea and I wish this Center success. But you should always remember that your long-term success depends on the success of the people of India as a whole and, therefore, one of the most important virtues to be cultivated today is commitment to the welfare of the people. I specially welcome your remark regarding respecting human dignity. We are a country where in spite of tremendous development and great progress, poverty and inequality still persist. And when we keep the problems of these people in the forefront and think of their dignity and their basic needs, then indeed we can create goodwill and sense of security in our own country and contribute to these concepts in the international field as well.

§ BANK NATIONALIZATION

Broadcast over All India Radio
[New Delhi, July 19, 1969]

Some of you have, perhaps, already heard that the Government has nationalized, by an ordinance, fourteen of the biggest commercial banks incorporated in India. I should like to tell you how we propose to operate the nationalized banking system.

As early as December 1954, Parliament took the decision to frame our plans and policies within a socialist pattern of society. Control over the commanding heights of the economy is necessary, particularly in a poor country where it is extremely difficult to mobilize adequate resources for development and to reduce the inequalities between different groups and regions. Ours is an ancient country but a young democracy, which has to remain ever vigilant to prevent the domination of the few over the social, economic or political systems.

Banks play a vital role in the functioning of any economy. To those who have money to spare, banks are the custodians of their savings, on which a good return can be earned by wise and efficient management. To the millions of small farmers, artisans and other self-employed persons, a bank can be a source of credit, which is the very basis for any effort to improve their meager economic lot. Even established trade and industry, big or small, cannot function or expand without adequate bank credit on reasonable terms. For our growing number of educated young men and women, banks offer an opportunity for employment, which at the same time is an opportunity for service to society. To those who do not have business of their own, banks, like the postal system or the railways, provide a facility for our daily life.

An institution, such as the banking system, which touches— and should touch—the lives of millions, has necessarily to be inspired by a larger social purpose and has to subserve national priorities and objectives. That is why there has been widespread demand that major banks should be not only socially controlled but publicly owned. It is not an accident that this has been the practice even in some countries which do not adhere to socialism. That is also why we nationalized, more than a decade ago, the life insurance business and the State Bank, or the Imperial Bank as it was then called. That is also why we have set up, directly under the aegis of the State, a number of financial institutions to provide medium or long-term credit to agriculture and industry. The step we have now taken is a continuation of the process which has long been under way. It is my earnest hope that it will mark a new and more vigorous phase in the implementation of our avowed plans and policies. But it is not the beginning of a new era of nationalization. Nor is it an attempt to transfer resources which are already employed productively to other sectors. The problems of growth, whether on farms or in factories, whether in backward regions or in others only relatively well-developed, whether in relation to exports or growing self-reliance, can be solved only in a positive manner, which looks essentially to an enlargement of resources and opportunities rather than to redistribution for its own sake. Certainly, public ownership of the major banks will help to eliminate the use of bank credit for speculative and unproductive purposes, particularly to the extent that it is encouraged at present by the association of a few leading groups with some of our major banks. I should like to assure all sections of industry and trade that legitimate needs for credit will be safeguarded. Indeed, it shall be our endeavor to ensure that bank credit expands on the basis of genuine savings in keeping with the growing needs of all productive sectors of the economy.

Some time ago we had adopted social control over banks. What is sought to be achieved through the present decision to nationalize the major banks is to accelerate the achievement of our objectives. The purpose of expanding bank credit to priority areas which have hitherto been somewhat neglected—such as (1) the removal of control by a few, (2) provision of adequate credit for agriculture, small industry and exports, (3) the giving of a professional bent to bank management, (4) the encouragement of new classes of entrepreneurs, (5) the provision of adequate training as well as reasonable terms of service for bank staff—still remains and will call for continuous efforts over a long time. Nationalization is necessary for the speedy achievement of these objectives. But the measure by itself will not achieve these objectives.

As far as possible, and certainly for some time to come, we propose to retain the separate identity and the present management of each bank. Therefore, when the banks reopen after the weekend, your relations with the bank will remain the same as they were before nationalization. This is true not only for those who bank in India, but also for those who bank abroad with the branches of the Indian banks which have now been taken over. In due course, structural and other changes may become necessary. These will be made in an orderly fashion and after broad-based consultations and the most detailed expert examination. Most of you are, perhaps, aware that a Banking Commission is examining this very problem of defining a structure for the banking system which would be more appropriate to the needs of the economy.

We are poised at present for substantial progress in agriculture and industry, in exports and in replacement of imports by domestic production. In order to exploit fully the opportunity which has been created by the enthusiasm and initiative of our farmers, workers, and industrialists, by the industrial capacity already built up and the growing cadres of well-trained managers and technicians, we must make a determined effort to mobilize resources and to deploy them wisely for productive uses. I have no doubt that the important step we have just taken, at the beginning of the new Plan period, will facilitate the achievement of the aspirations we all share for our great country.

I appeal to all of you to help in the productive and purposeful implementation of this step. I appeal particularly to the managers and staff of the banks, which have been nationalized, to cooperate fully in the task of making the banking system serve our national objectives better. I am sure that the management and the staff of these banks will make every effort to render prompt and courteous service to those whose well-earned savings are entrusted to their care.

In our internal as in foreign policy, we believe in acting according to our judgment and in keeping with our traditions and needs. There can be no question of aligning ourselves this way or that, whether internally or externally. We remain committed to the freedom and progress of the people of this great country.

Address in Parliament
[New Delhi, August 7, 1969]

This debate in the House has revealed many strange things—
the people who support the bill and why they support it, those
who do not support and the reasons for which they do not support—and many strange arguments, theories and similes have been
put forth. Whatever the reasons, I should like to express my grati-
tude for the general support which Honorable Members have extended to this bill. I have already expressed my thoughts on it here
and most of the points which have been made have already been
dealt with previously.

However, I should like to remind the House that it was more
than a decade ago that Parliament put before the country the goal
of a socialist pattern of society. To us this did not imply ownership
of all the means of production by the State, but we did visualize
that there should be large areas for the operation of private initiative and enterprise subject always to regulation in the public interest. The socialist pattern of society did impose on us the obligation
to bring the strategic areas of our economy under State ownership
and control. It also meant that the Government had and has an
obligation to take remedial measures to ensure that our political
democracy is not eroded by economic distortions.

In every country, including the predominantly capitalist communities, it has been recognized that banks and other financial institutions occupy a vital position. In an economy such as ours,
which is a developing one and which is seeking to compress the
process of development within the span of a few five-year plans, the
role of banks is even more important than in the mature economies. We must stimulate the saving habit amongst all sections of
our people, both in the rural and the urban areas. We must see
that these savings are garnered and utilized in accordance with the
priorities and objectives of our Plans, and in our new Plan, on
which we have just embarked, we want to provide greater opportunities for small and new entrepreneurs. We want to ensure that the
full potentialities of the agricultural revolution, which is under
way in many parts of the country, are realized and that the efforts
and aspirations of our progressive farmers are not impeded for want

of credit. We want to initiate corrective action against the concentration of economic power and privilege which has come about in the wake of economic development.

We cannot deny that the control of the banking system by the bigger business groups was an important contributory factor in the growth of monopolies in the private sector. In spite of all the publicized efficiency of the private banking system over all these years, we find that deposits in them constitute only 16 percent of the national income and I understand—I think this point has been made by other Honorable Members—that there are still thirteen districts in India where there is not a single banking office and the major metropolitan centers still account for the bulk of bank deposits and bank credit. Can anyone deny that the development of banking facilities has been lopsided and that banks have not been efficient instruments in the mobilization of deposits and the provision of credit for worthwhile purposes in different parts of our country?

I do not want to embark on the virtues or otherwise of the public sector. I should like to say, however, that in the field of banking, the public sector has a record of which it can be legitimately proud. I see my Honorable friend, Shri Babubhai Chinai, here and I would, therefore, like to say a few words specifically about the State Bank. I think it has shown imagination and initiative in formulating and implementing programs to finance small-scale industries since 1956. At the end of 1968, the total sanctioned limits for assistance to small-scale industrial units by the State Bank and its subsidiaries amounted to Rs. 162 crore.

The State Bank also played an important part in providing remittance facilities. In 1969 alone remittances effected through the State Bank on behalf of the cooperative banks which are dispersed throughout the country amounted to nearly Rs. 700 crores. Also the State Bank, from the very beginning, looked upon the provision of banking facilities in the rural areas and semiurban areas to be one of its primary responsibilities. More than 70 percent of the branches opened by the State Bank and its subsidiaries were in towns with a population of less than 25,000. About 60 percent of the total number of branches are today located in such smaller places.

The State Bank has also been a pioneer in introducing several new facilities. Some of these are: travelers' checks, credit transfers, installment credit scheme for the benefit of small-scale industries, one-man offices and schemes for assisting qualified technicians, transport operators and retail trade. The State Bank has undertaken these developmental activities without detriment to commercial and banking principles. Its record in the mobilization of deposits compares favorably with other banks.

Now, this is where I come to Shri Chinai. In 1968, the State Bank's deposits rose by 12 percent. Its performance was better than that of other banks. Shri Chinai observed that while the deposits of the State Bank rose only by 84 percent during 1960–68, the deposits of the other scheduled banks in the private sector went up by 164 percent. Now, why has this happened? This does not accurately reflect the growth of public deposits in the State Bank because at the end of December 1960 the aggregate deposits with the State Bank were Rs. 576 crore, out of which PL-480 deposits were Rs. 241 crore. The PL-480 deposits were subsequently transferred to the Reserve Bank of India over the next two or three years, of course, under a phased program. Therefore, if we exclude the PL-480 deposits, public deposits in the State Bank rose from Rs. 335 crore—that is, Rs. 576 crore minus Rs. 241 crore—to Rs. 1061 crore at the end of December 1968. This reflects a rise of about 200 percent. So, it is clear that we have allowed the State Bank to function untrammeled, without interference by the Government on political or other considerations and I think this should give sufficient assurance to this House and the people at large that the banks which we have taken over will function not as wings of the Government, but as sound business institutions.

There is one point I would like to make very strongly and that is that sound business does not mean that credit should be provided only to those who can furnish security in the form of property and that it should be denied to others even if the projects proposed by them are otherwise credit-worthy. I think that the whole emphasis should shift from credit-worthiness of persons to the credit-worthiness of purpose.

Loans which help production and in stimulating employment will now be encouraged, while borrowing for speculation and similar purposes will be discouraged. Today our banks are not well equipped to deal with loan applications on the basis of their viability. Government will take early steps to arrange for intensive training of personnel for technical appraisal of projects, and in view of nationalization it will be possible to pool the resources of the fourteen banks and to promote programs of training on a common basis.

I have said several times and I should like to repeat that nationalization does not mean that the existing industrial enterprises will be deprived of their credit needs for genuine productive purposes. But we are aware that there is a tendency on the part of some enterprises to make heavy demands on bank resources while their own internal resources are used for other purposes such as cornering shares and acquiring control over other enterprises; these practices, I am sure the House will agree, must be curbed.

May I also emphasize that nationalization will lead to a more equitable distribution of credit throughout the country. Honorable Members are aware that many areas of our country have remained backward not for want of natural resources, but for various historical reasons. It is our duty to ensure that their backwardness is not perpetuated for want of finance. Now with nationalization, it will be possible to draw up a rationalized program of expansion which will pay special attention to those States and those parts of the country which have so far lagged behind. Institutions providing finance for the development of industries have recently decided to take certain steps to encourage enterprises in backward areas and the nationalized banks must provide working capital and contribute to the growth of industries in these backward regions.

It is unfortunate that even some responsible persons and some people even in Parliament should try to create misgivings and a sense of insecurity amongst the depositors. I should like to repeat the assurance, if indeed it is needed at all, that the interests of the depositors will always be kept in the forefront and they may rest assured that their funds in the nationalized banks are safe as those in the State Bank of India or in the Post Office Savings Banks.

Critics forget that small savers in our country have long been used to putting their money in Post Office Savings Banks for nearly a century, and State Bank has already more than a decade of loyal service to its credit. I am sure that the depositors will not pay heed to the criticism of the self-appointed guardians of their interest. Their true guardian is the Government, and efficiency and courtesy should be the watchword of our nationalized banks. Special responsibility, of course, rests not only with the Government, but also with the employees of the banks, including the supervisory and managerial staff. I have no doubt that the professional and managerial staff will rise to the occasion, as it now has a unique opportunity to promote the real interests of the community through sincere and dedicated service. I have faith in the innate good sense of the employees of the public sector, and I am sure that this faith will be fully vindicated in their performance in the years to come.

May I add that the large numbers who have been coming to see me have, of their own accord, assured me of their cooperation in this matter. I should like to request businessmen and industrialists to adopt nationalization not merely in the spirit of acquiescing in an accomplished fact but of extending their hand of cooperation in developing our economy. May I remind them that the Government and they have a vital common interest in accelerating economic growth through progressive and coordinated endeavor. There is still considerable room for free play and to provide them with initiative and drive in many fields. So, I hope that instead of adopting a purely negative, critical attitude towards the policies of the Government, they will realize their obligation towards the society and walk with the Government towards the fulfillment of the objectives which are enshrined in our Plan.

I think there has been no single measure the Government has taken in recent years which has evoked such widespread approval. Not only farmers, small-scale industrialists, trade unionists and professional and managerial classes have welcomed it both for its intrinsic merit and for the evidence it affords of Government's concern for social justice and economic growth, but many other people have also been coming, and, if I may say so, the shift which was visible between the stand taken by the Jan Sangh in the other House and the stand taken by it in this House is itself a proof or witness that within these few days even they, isolated as they are from the contemporary world by the cobweb of superstition and of communalism, must pay some heed to the upsurge of feeling which they see all round them.

The Swatantra Party's thinking we have always seen to be a little twisted, and how twisted it is has been demonstrated once again. I would like to ask the House only one question: Is the right of a person to put money into a particular bank greater than the right of the common man to basic necessities which right also is enshrined in our Constitution? We all have rights. We all have needs. But there must be some comparison. Some years ago when I paid a state visit to the United States, I quoted a proverb which I believe comes from Maharashtra: "A man said, 'I complained that I had no shoes until I met the man who had no feet.' " We have to look at the problems of the country from that angle. Nobody wants to deny the rights of any person unless these rights are impinging on far more valid rights of a far larger number. This is the question which is put before us. It may also interest the Honorable Members that after I said that 95 percent of the public has supported the measure, besides the large numbers of associations, labor, peasants, rickshawallas and stone-cutters and others who came to me, a very large number of people have written or come from the intelligentsia, including bankers, editors, depositors, and so forth, assuring me that they would like to be counted within the 95 percent. It is for the Honorable Members to judge whether—this point I think has been made, I cannot remember by whom—chaos is more likely to come because of some slight annoyance or slight inconvenience to a few people than from the disturbance and tension which the growing disparity causes amongst vast numbers of the underprivileged in our country.

Some Honorable Members here and many people outside have raised the bogey of communism. It is strange to see that Mc-Carthyism, which is long dead in the place of its birth, should have now found a foothold across the seas and the continents in India. It shows that those who propound this theory show an astounding ignorance of the political forces at work in our country and of the facts of life in the India of 1969. I was astonished to see screaming headlines in some financial newspapers about a speech which I made recently. I said nothing in that speech which I have not been saying for many years, when I was Congress President, after that and before that, and I think that this is a very deliberate attempt to distort and misrepresent the thought or feelings or sort of views which I was trying to put across to the people who had gathered. Certainly, I said that many changes have to take place. Is there anybody here who will say that we do not want changes in this country? What are we sitting here for? What is the Government functioning for?

It is the business of every one of us who is responsible, who is at all interested in the welfare of the country, to see that the country changes steadily and as fast as possible because the people's impatience is growing. It has already been said, I have said it, that this is a small step we have taken. I do not think it is a giant step or revolutionary step, but it is a small, very definite step in a particular direction, and what I said there was that if we did not implement this step or if we did not do all the follow-up which was necessary, then this step would be worthless. This is what I said. This is what I believe in. Many things have to be changed in our country. The whole picture of disparity has to be changed. I do not think this has anything to do even with socialism. This is just plain common sense.

Therefore, we should not get swept off our feet or like King Canute try to control the waves and say that if we want the sea to stop at a particular place, it will stop. Here the sea is a mass of human beings, human beings who are politically conscious, human beings who have suffered and struggled for freedom and who today are suffering and struggling to make that freedom real.

It is not in the power of Honorable Members opposite nor is it in my power to stop this upsurge of public feeling. No one can have missed the tremendous psychological change which has come about in this country by this one small step. I do not think that anybody, even the least understanding, even the poorest person, thinks that this is going to change his life suddenly or that it is some miraculous wand which has been waved. They are very conscious that it is not. But they think that at last things are moving and they think that we were in a rut and we have got out of the rut. How far we move, where we move, that responsibility is still with us. But they do think that we have been able to push back the forces of inertia and of *status quo*. Nowhere else is this change of mood and exhilaration more noticeable than in my own party. Congressmen who live at the grass-roots level feel that bank nationalization is the fulfillment of larger goals and objectives of our party to which its leaders pledged themselves even in the thick of the struggle for freedom decades ago. It is an important step forward in keeping with its promise to the people and in keeping with the changing needs of the time. If I may, I want to quote something:

I am afraid that for years to come India would be engaged in passing legislations in order to raise the down-trodden, the fallen from the mire into which they have been sunk by the capitalists, by the landlords, by the so-called higher classes. If we are to relieve these people from the mire, then it would be the bounden duty of the national Government of India in order to set its house in order continually to give preference to these people and free them from the burdens under which they are being crushed.

This is not a Communist speaking; it is Mahatma Gandhi.

Some Honorable Member, I think my good friend Shri S. N. Mishra, expressed fears regarding the likely political appointments. Now, "politics" again, is a word with strange and different meanings. When I was in England a long time ago—I was a student—we heard the phrase "the politics of the unpolitical," which is that any change in the existing state of affairs is considered "political" but if a person sticks to the *status quo* and fights the forces of change, that is considered to be "unpolitical." Only the other day, I read a well-known, non-Communist liberal British journal. In this there was a description of the typical double standard which exists. That is "Radical rules are called doctrinaire meddling while *status quo,* right-wing rules are supposed to be the free man's commonsense." Similar confused thinking seems to persist in our country also.

Bank nationalization, as I have said earlier, is but a part, a significant part of our larger program. May I say, because of these headlines which have been appearing in the newspapers, that there is no mystery or hidden surprise about our future program. Our policies and our programs have always been open, have always been in front of the people. The broad socialist objectives which my party seeks to serve and which we have placed before Parliament have been approved by Parliament. Nationalization of banks was intended to serve the same goal. Other aspects of our programs have been incorporated in our Plans and in the economic policy which our great party has approved. They were summed up recently in a resolution adopted unanimously by my party at Bangalore. These are the items of the program; they have to be studied in depth and pursued.

Today we have taken one step. We have to see that it is properly and rightly implemented. But we shall certainly look at the other programs which the party has endorsed. What is needed at this moment is a new sense of urgency, a new sense of dynamism, a new sense of dedication and service. Let us make this the occasion. After a long time we have such a large commitment to this program, with support almost from every political party with the exception of two, and from the country at large. This can form the basis for our cooperation in taking our country in the right direction, not at once but certainly step by step. It will take us out of the present stagnation towards a better and brighter future.

§ THE HUMAN ENVIRONMENT

Address to the United Nations Conference on
the Human Environment
[Stockholm, June 14, 1972]

It is indeed an honor to address this conference—in itself a fresh expression of the spirit which created the United Nations—concern for the present and future welfare of humanity. It does not aim merely at securing limited agreements but at establishing peace and harmony in life—among all races and with nature. This gathering represents man's earnest endeavor to understand his own condition and to prolong his tenancy of this planet. A vast amount of detailed preparatory work has gone into the convening of this conference guided by the dynamic personality of Mr. Maurice Strong, Secretary-General of the conference.

I have had the good fortune of growing up with a sense of kinship with nature in all its manifestations. Birds, plants, stones were companions and, sleeping under the star-strewn sky, I became familiar with the names and movements of the constellations.

But my deep interest in this our "only earth" was not for itself but as a fit home for man.

One cannot be truly human and civilized unless one looks upon not only all fellowmen but all creation with the eyes of a friend. Throughout India, edicts carved on rocks and iron pillars are reminders that twenty-two centuries ago the Emperor Ashoka defined a king's duty as not merely to protect citizens and punish wrongdoers, but also to preserve animal life and forest trees. Ashoka was the first and perhaps the only monarch until very recently to forbid the killing of a large number of species of animals for sport or food, foreshadowing some of the concerns of this conference. He went further, regretting the carnage of his military conquests and enjoining upon his successors to find "their only pleasure in the peace that comes through righteousness."

Along with the rest of mankind, we in India—in spite of Ashoka—have been guilty of wanton disregard for the sources of our sustenance. We share your concern at the rapid deterioration of flora and fauna. Some of our own wildlife has been wiped out; miles of forests with beautiful old trees, mute witnesses of history, have been destroyed. Even though our industrial development is in its infancy, and at its most difficult stage, we are taking various steps to deal with incipient environmental imbalances. The more so because of our concern for the human being—a species which is also imperiled. In poverty he is threatened by malnutrition and disease, in weakness by war, in richness by the pollution brought about by his own prosperity.

It is sad that in country after country, progress should become synonymous with an assault on nature. We who are a part of nature and dependent on her for every need speak constantly about "exploiting" nature. When the highest mountain in the world was climbed in 1953, Jawaharlal Nehru objected to the phrase "conquest of Everest" which he thought was arrogant. Is it surprising that this lack of consideration and the constant need to prove one's superiority should be projected onto our treatment of our fellowmen? I remember Edward Thompson, a British writer and a good friend of India, once telling Mr. Gandhi that wildlife was fast disappearing. Remarked the Mahatma— "It is decreasing in the jungles but it is increasing in the towns!"

We are gathered here under the aegis of the United Nations.

We are supposed to belong to the same family, sharing common traits and impelled by the same basic desires, yet we inhabit a divided world.

How can it be otherwise? There is still no recognition of the equality of man or respect for him as an individual. In matters of color and race, religion and custom, society is governed by prejudice. Tensions arise because of man's aggressiveness and notions of superiority. The power of the big stick prevails and it is used not in favor of fair play or beauty, but to chase imaginary windmills— to assume the right to interfere in the affairs of others, and to arrogate authority for action which would not normally be allowed. Many of the advanced countries of today have reached their present affluence by their domination over other races and countries, the exploitation of their own masses and their own natural resources. They got a head start through sheer ruthlessness, undisturbed by feelings of compassion or by abstract theories of freedom, equality or justice. The stirrings of demands for the political rights of citizens, and the economic rights of the toiler came after considerable advance had been made. The riches and the labor of the colonized countries played no small part in the industrialization and prosperity of the West. Now, as we struggle to create a better life for our people, it is vastly different circumstances, for obviously in today's eagle-eyed watchfulness, we cannot indulge in such practices even for a worthwhile purpose. We are bound by our own ideals. We owe allegiance to the principles of the rights of workers and the norms enshrined in the charters of international organizations. Above all, we are answerable to the millions of politically awakened citizens in our countries. All these make progress costlier and more complicated.

On the one hand the rich look askance at our continuing poverty—on the other they warn us against their own methods. We do not wish to impoverish the environment any further and yet we cannot for a moment forget the grim poverty of large numbers of people. Are not poverty and need the greatest polluters? For instance, unless we are in a position to provide employment and purchasing power for the daily necessities of the tribal people and those who live in or around our jungles, we cannot prevent them from combing the forest for food and livelihood, from poaching and from despoiling the vegetation. When they themselves feel deprived, how can we urge the preservation of animals? How can we speak to those who live in villages and in slums about keeping the oceans, the rivers and the air clean when their own lives are contaminated at the source? The environment cannot be improved in conditions of poverty. Nor can poverty be eradicated without the use of science and technology.

Must there be conflict between technology and a truly better world or between enlightenment of the spirit and a higher standard of living? Foreigners sometimes ask what to us seems a very strange question, whether progress in India would not mean a diminishing of her spirituality or her values. Is spiritual quality so superficial as to be dependent upon the lack of material comfort? As a country we are no more or less spiritual than any other, but traditionally our people have respected the spirit of detachment and renunciation. Historically, our great spiritual discoveries were made during periods of comparative affluence. The doctrines of detachment from possessions were developed not as rationalization of deprivation but to prevent comfort and ease from dulling the senses. Spirituality means the enrichment of the spirit, the strengthening of one's inner resources and the stretching of one's range of experience. It is the ability to be still in the midst of activity and vibrantly alive in moments of calm; to separate the essence from circumstances; to accept joy and sorrow with some equanimity. Perception and compassion are the marks of true spirituality.

I am reminded of an incident in one of our tribal areas. The vociferous demand of elder tribal chiefs that their customs should be left undisturbed found support from noted anthropologists. In its anxiety that the majority should not submerge the many ethnical racial and cultural groups in our country, the Government of India largely accepted this advice. I was amongst those who entirely approved. However, a visit to a remote part of our northeast frontier brought me in touch with a different point of view—the protest of the younger elements that while the rest of India was on the way to modernization they were being preserved as museum pieces. Could we not say the same to the affluent nations?

For the last quarter of a century, we have been engaged in an enterprise unparalleled in human history—the provision of basic needs to one-sixth of mankind within the span of one or two generations. When we launched on that effort our early planners had more than the usual gaps to fill. There were not enough data and no helpful books. No guidance could be sought from the experience of other countries whose conditions—political, economic, social and technological—were altogether different. Planning in the sense we were innovating had never been used in the context of a mixed economy. But we could not wait. The need to improve the conditions of our people was pressing. Planning and action, improvement of data leading to better planning and better action, all this was a continuous and overlapping process. Our industrialization tended to follow the paths which the more advanced countries had traversed earlier. With the advance of the sixties and particularly during the last five years, we have encountered a bewildering collection of problems, some due to our shortcomings but many inherent in the process and in existing attitudes. The feeling is growing that we should reorder our priorities and move away from the single-dimensional model which has viewed growth from certain limited angles, which seems to have given a higher place to things rather than to persons and which has increased our wants rather than our enjoyment. We should have a more comprehensive approach to life, centered on man not as a statistic but an individual with many sides to his personality. The solution of these problems cannot be isolated phenomena of marginal importance but must be an integral part of the unfolding of the very process of development.

The extreme forms in which questions of population or environmental pollution are posed obscure the total view of political, economic and social situations. The Government of India is one of the few which has an officially sponsored program of family planning and this is making some progress. We believe that planned families will make for a healthier and more conscious population. But we know also that no program of population control can be effective without education and without a visible rise in the standard of living. Our own programs have succeeded in the urban or semiurban areas. To the very poor, every child is an earner and a helper. We are experimenting with new approaches, and the family planning program is being combined with those of maternity and child welfare, nutrition and development in general.

It is an oversimplification to blame all the world's problems on increasing population. Countries with but a small fraction of the world population consume the bulk of the world's production of minerals, fossil fuels and so on. Thus we see that when it comes to the depletion of natural resources and environmental pollution, the increase of one inhabitant in an affluent country, at his level of living, is equivalent to an increase of many Asians, Africans or Latin Americans as their current material levels of living.

The inherent conflict is not between conservation and development, but between environment and the reckless exploitation of man and earth in the name of efficiency. Historians tell us that the modern age began with the will to freedom of the individual. And the individual came to believe that he had rights with no corresponding obligations. The man who got ahead was the one who commanded admiration. No questions were asked as to the methods employed or the price which others had had to pay. The industrial civilization has promoted the concept of the efficient man, he whose entire energies are concentrated on producing more in a given unit of time and from a given unit of man power. Groups or individuals who are less competitive and, according to this test, less efficient are regarded as lesser breeds—for example the older civilizations, the black and brown peoples, women and certain professions. Obsolescence is built into production, and efficiency is based on the creation of goods which are not really needed and which cannot be disposed of, when discarded. What price such efficiency now, and is not reckless a more appropriate term for such behavior?

All the "isms" of the modern age—even those which in theory disown the private profit principle—assume that man's cardinal interest is acquisition. The profit motive, individual or collective, seems to overshadow all else. This overriding concern with self and today is the basic cause of the ecological crisis.

Pollution is not a technical problem. The fault lies not in science and technology as such but in the sense of values of the contemporary world which ignores the rights of others and is oblivious of the longer perspective.

There are grave misgivings that the discussion on ecology may be designed to distract attention from the problems of war and poverty. We have to prove to the disinherited majority of the world that ecology and conservation will not work against their interest but will bring an improvement in their lives. To withhold technology from them would deprive them of vast resources of energy and knowledge. This is no longer feasible nor will it be acceptable.

The environmental problems of developing countries are not the side effects of excessive industrialization but reflect the inadequacy of development. The rich countries may look upon development as the cause of environmental destruction, but to us it is one of the primary means of improving the environment for living, or providing food, water, sanitation and shelter, of making the deserts green and the mountains habitable. The research and perseverance of dedicated people have given us an insight which is likely to play an important part in the shaping of our future plans. We see that however much man hankers after material goods, they can never give him full satisfaction. Thus the higher standard of living must be achieved without alienating people from their heritage and without despoiling nature of its beauty, freshness and purity so essential to our lives.

The most urgent and basic question is that of peace. Nothing is so pointless as modern warfare. Nothing destroys so instantly, so completely, as the diabolic weapons which not only kill but maim and deform the living and the yet to be born; which poison the land, leaving long trails of ugliness, barrenness and hopeless desolation. What ecological project can survive a war? The Prime Minister of Sweden, Mr. Olof Palme, has already drawn the attention of the Conference to this in powerful words.

It is clear that the environmental crisis which is confronting the world will profoundly alter the future destiny of our planet. No one among us, whatever our status, strength of circumstance, can remain unaffected. The process of change challenges present international policies. Will the growing awareness of "one earth" and "one environment" guide us to the concept of "one humanity"? Will there be more equitable sharing of environmental costs and greater international interest in the accelerated progress of the less developed world? Or will it remain confined to a narrow concern, based on exclusive self-sufficiency?

The first essays in narrowing economic and technological disparities have not succeeded because the policies of aid were made to subserve the equations of power. We hope that the renewed emphasis on self-reliance, brought about by the change in the climate for aid, will also promote a search for new criteria of human satisfaction. In the meantime, the ecological crisis should not add to the burdens of the weaker nations by introducing new considerations in the political and trade policies of rich nations. It would be ironic if the fight against pollution were to be converted into another business, out of which a few companies, corporations, or nations would make profits at the cost of the many. Here is a branch of experimentation and discovery in which scientists of all nations should take interest. They should ensure that their findings are available to all nations, restricted by patents. I am glad that the conference has given thought on this aspect of the problem.

Life is one and the world is one, and all these questions are interlinked. The population explosion, poverty, ignorance and disease, the pollution of our surroundings, the stockpiling of nuclear weapons and biological and chemical agents of destruction are all parts of a vicious circle. Each is important and urgent, but dealing with them one by one would be wasted effort.

It serves little purpose to dwell on the past or to apportion blame, for none of us is blameless. If some are able to dominate over others, this is at least partially due to the weakness, the lack of unity and the temptation of gaining some advantage on the part of those who submit. If the prosperous have been exploiting the needy, can we honestly claim that in our own societies, people do not take advantage of the weaker sections? We must reevaluate the fundamentals in which our respective civic societies are based and the ideals by which they are sustained. If there is to be change of heart, a change of direction and methods of functioning, it is not an organization or a country—no matter how well intentioned—which can achieve it. While each country must deal with that aspect of the problem which is most relevant to it, it is obvious that all countries must unite in an overall endeavor. There is no alternative to a cooperative approach on a global scale to the entire spectrum of our problems.

I have referred to some problems which seem to me to be the underlying causes of the present crises in our civilization. This is not in the expectation that this conference can achieve miracles or solve all the world's difficulties, but in the hope that the opinions of each nation will be kept in focus, that these problems will be viewed in perspective and each project devised as part of the whole.

On a previous occasion I have spoken of the unfinished revolution in our countries. I am now convinced that this can be taken to its culmination when it is accompanied by a revolution in social thinking. In 1968 at the 14th General Conference of UNESCO, the Indian delegation, along with others, proposed a new and major program entitled "a design for living." This is essential to grasp the full implications of technical advance and its impact on different sections and groups. We do not want to put the clock back or resign ourselves to a simplistic natural state. We want new directions in the wiser use of the knowledge and tools with which science has equipped us. And this cannot be just one upsurge but a continuous search into cause and effect and an unending effort to match technology with higher levels of thinking. We must concern ourselves not only with the kind of worlds we want, but also with what kind of man should inhabit it. Surely we do not desire a society divided into those who are conditioned and those who are not conditioned. We want thinking people, capable of spontaneous, self-directed activity, people who are interested and interesting, and who are imbued with compassion and concern for others.

It will not be easy for large societies to change their style of living. They cannot be coerced to do so, nor can governmental action suffice. People can be motivated and urged to participate in better alternatives.

It has been my experience that people who are at cross-purposes with nature are cynical about mankind and ill at ease with themselves. Modern man must reestablish an unbroken link with nature and with life. He must again learn to invoke the energy of growing things and to recognize, as did the ancients in India centuries ago, that one can take from the earth and the atmosphere only so much as one puts back into them. In their hymn to earth, the sages of the Atharva Veda chanted, I quote:

> What of thee I dig out, let that quickly grow over,
> Let me not hit thy vitals, or thy heart.

So can man himself be vital and of good heart and conscious of his responsibility.

part 2
INDIA AND THE WORLD

India and
the United States of America

Address at dinner given by President Lyndon B. Johnson
[Washington, March 28, 1966]

Your words, Mr. President, were exceedingly moving. You have spoken of India and her wide variety. We who live there are naturally deeply conscious of it; at the same time we are fully aware of the underlying unity which binds together all our people.

You quoted some words of my father. I should like to quote something you have said. You said, Mr. President, that "Reality rarely matches dreams, but only dreams give nobility to purpose." In the United States, you have matched your dreams in many ways. Yet you still seek, and rightly, to offer the American people a better and more purposeful life. You have called this idea "The Great Society." In India we have our dreams which may seem trite to you who sit here because they are so simple—food barely sufficient to keep one from hunger; shelter to keep out the wind and the rain; medicine and education by which to restore the faith and the hope of nearly five hundred million people.

But everything in life is relative. There is an old proverb in my country. A person says, "I complained that I had no shoes until I met a man who had no feet."

Mahatma Gandhi once said, and it is something which my father often repeated, that we in India had to work to wipe the tear

from every eye. That, of course, is a big task, and I doubt if it can
be done in any country. And yet we have been trying to do that for
eighteen long years. Two centuries of subjugation cannot be
washed away so easily. It takes time. It takes work. It takes
courage. India is changing. . . . Nowhere in the world can the
contrast be so striking. We have not only different levels of development between the different States, but even within each State we
have often several centuries existing side by side. We have some of
the greatest irrigation works in the world and yet, in parts of our
State of Rajasthan in the desert, families store precious water under
lock and key. During a tour of some of these border areas a couple
of months or so ago, I myself experienced the great hardship of
doing without water and measuring the miles from well to well.

Some twelve million or more of bullock carts still churn the
dust of our village roads. Yet, in other parts of India, we are building three nuclear power plants.

Average agricultural yields are low. At the same time there are
areas where we obtain sugar-cane yields that compare favorably
with those in Hawaii or in Java.

A third of the illiterate people in the world are in India. Yet,
we are steadily conquering illiteracy. In our State of Maharashtra,
village after village strives to achieve total literacy. Parents learn
from their children so that the honor of the village is upheld. In
Madras, people have banded together to improve their schools.
They have given one hundred million rupees beyond what the
Government spends on their schools. In the Punjab, little work-
shops make lathes and pumps that have revolutionized the countryside.

The seeming inconsistencies and conflicts of India are legion.
The setbacks—and we have had many—are heartbreaking. Yet the
signs of change are clear and constantly growing.

Sometimes critics point to an example of success and say, "This
proves nothing. This is a mere drop in the ocean of Indian poverty." How wrong this is. For every success reinforces the prospect
of further success. It shows that success is possible.

This is really our major problem. Years ago, when we visited
the villages to persuade people to try for a better life, they turned
to us and said, "There can be no better life. God wills it this way.

This is our lot and we have to suffer it." Today, not a single voice will be heard like this. There is only one demand, the demand for a better life. This, in itself, I think, is a very big achievement.

You talked of democracy. May I tell you a story which I shared with the Vice-President a short while ago? It happened during our first election. I had gone to speak in a village where, just the day before, the leader of an opposition party had spoken. When my speech ended, an elderly gentleman got up from the audience and said, "We have listened very carefully to what you have said, but just the day before somebody came and he said exactly the opposite. Now, which one of you was telling the truth?"

This, you can understand, is an extremely tricky question to ask a public speaker. I said, "Well, I think that what I said was the truth, but I have no doubt that the gentleman thought that what he said was the truth. The whole point of democracy is that everybody should say what he thinks is the truth and you, the people, have to judge whose is the correct version and which is the right thing for you."

Well, this was rather a difficult explanation for them, so they said, "Now, you tell us, do you belong to the Congress Party?" I said, "I do." "Is your party in power? Is it forming the Government?" I said, "Yes, it is." "Then what business have you to send somebody here who tells us incorrect things? It is your business to keep him away."

This was one of the stops where I was supposed to stay only ten minutes, but I stayed two hours trying to argue the whole point about elections, freedom of expression, and so on. I cannot say that I got any further at the end of the two hours.

But now, years later, we find that we have got further. Nobody in India today would put such a question. Everyone knows that different parties have their points of view; that these points of view are put before the people to judge; and that the people judge, not always rightly, but at least they try to judge rightly. Certainly, from election to election, they have shown a great maturity.

India very definitely is on the move. The United States has given us valuable assistance in our struggle against poverty, hunger, ignorance and disease. We are grateful for this act of friendship. But we also know that our own "Great Society" must and can rest securely only on the quality and extent of our own effort. This effort we are determined to make. We owe it to our friends; and even more so, we owe it to ourselves.

Nevertheless, I believe that it is of the greatest importance, to use your own words, to bring into closer union the spirit and courage of both our countries. I welcome your intention to set up an Indo-American Foundation which will give tangible shape and form to this union.

The present-day world offers the possibility of bringing together one people with another. The young men and women of your Peace Corps are well known and well loved in our country. Every endeavor to sustain and enlarge this people-to-people partnership is a good effort and is welcome.

Friendship with America is not a new thing for us. Those of us in India who have been involved with the struggle for freedom have known, from our earliest days, your own struggle here. We have been taught the words of your leaders and of your past great Presidents. Above all, we were linked because of the friendship and understanding that President Roosevelt showed us during some of the most difficult days of our independence struggle. I have no doubt that the friendly advice given by him to the British Government facilitated and accelerated our freedom.

But there again the major effort had to be our own. Even today, we want to bear our burden and we are doing so, but a little help is welcome from friends who consider it worthwhile to lighten our burden. India's problems today are her own, but they are also the world's problems. India, if it is stable, united and democratic, can serve a great purpose. If India is not stable, if India fails, it would be a failure of the whole democratic system. It would be a failure of many of the values which you and I hold dear. That is why, Mr. President, I welcome your words and I welcome this meeting with you.

From address at dinner given by the Economic Club
[New York, March 30, 1966]

I come to the United States and to New York not as a stranger but as a friend. New York is the financial and cultural center of your great country and I am aware that your club is one of the best known groups in the business and banking community of this city. I am especially pleased, therefore, to be with you this evening.

My theme today is the performance and prospects of the Indian economy, a subject in which, I know, you have long been interested. The basic fact about India is that she is at once a very old and a very young country. She has had a long history, a great culture and many traditions. But it is less than eighteen years since she emerged into her own from the shackles of colonial rule. With the winning of freedom, we lost no time in adopting for ourselves a program of economic development. Our first Five Year Plan was launched in 1951. In a few days, we shall complete the third of these Five Year Plans and fifteen years of development will be behind us. This period of time, so full of performance and achievements as well as of rising but unfulfilled expectations, is a useful time-frame for taking stock.

The recorded facts of progress are certainly impressive in all spheres of economic activity—agriculture, industry, infrastructure, health and education. I shall not repeat them in detail. Yet I cannot resist quoting some figures which will give you a broad-brush picture of what has taken place in India. In these fifteen years, the production of food grains went up from 50 to 88 million tons. Industrial production has been steadily rising at the rate of 7 to 8 percent per annum. The capacity for generation of electricity has increased five-fold from 1.7 million kilowatts in 1950 to 8.5 million kilowatts in 1965. Nearly 70 million children attend school today, as against 25 million in 1950. Malaria and smallpox have been eradicated and the expectation of life has increased from 32 years in the 1940s to 50 years now.

In this tremendous endeavor, India has been greatly helped by her friends abroad. We are grateful for the generosity and understanding with which this help has been forthcoming. Our own efforts in mobilizing domestic savings have also been very substantial. In a country as poor as India, where the margin between income and consumption is necessarily narrow, it is rather remarkable that domestic savings have doubled from 5 percent of the national income in 1951 to over 11 percent in 1966. In the last fifteen years, these internal savings have financed 80 percent of our total investment. With patience and good cheer, our people have accepted the growing role of taxation in financing the rapidly expanding programs for development and social services. As another measure of self-reliance, exports in the last five years have increased at the rate of 5 percent per annum. The doctrine of self-help is, therefore, not by any means new to us. From the very beginning, we have been committed to and have steadily organized ourselves for self-reliance to as large a degree as possible.

The practical connotation which we have given to this concept of self-reliance is to undertake, early in the process of development, basic investments designed to exploit fully our human and material resources. We have built steel mills, not because they are prestigious but because India has vast reserves of good iron ore and skilled and inexpensive labor. We can produce steel cheaply. We are organized for fabricating machinery and for designing plants using our own steel. We have coal, oil and bauxite which we have proceeded to exploit in the same way. Qualitatively, the last fifteen years have seen not only a growth but a diversification and sophistication of the industrial structure of India. This has meant that we now increasingly import raw materials and components. In many key commodities, the proportion of imports to total consumption is steadily going down.

I am sure you cannot be unaware of these broad facts. But, unfortunately, this is not the picture which has been in the forefront of world news about India in recent months. That is why I wished to draw your attention to them once again this evening.

In recent months, in India as well as outside, there has been much public discussion on the strains which have developed in the Indian economy. It is not my purpose to take you through the detailed causes which have contributed to the phase of strain and tension which admittedly we are experiencing today. It seems to me that much of our present difficulties in regard to food and foreign exchange are, in a large part, a reflection of the fact that the rising expectations of the Indian people have overtaken the progress so far achieved. The greatest single lesson to be drawn is that in future plans we should aim to achieve decisively higher results than we have done so far.

In this context, the crucial sector is clearly agriculture. Over the last fifteen years, Indian agriculture has grown up nearly 4 percent per annum. The demand has simultaneously gone up, due not only to the increase in population but also because people eat more, prefer better food and live longer. Even so, with the agricultural growth we have achieved, production might have been adequate for meeting our minimum requirements if only food could be steadily produced without any fluctuations beyond the control of man. Unfortunately, the vicissitudes of weather have greater impact in India than perhaps in other parts of the world. We have a high proportion of arable land, but less than a fifth of it is irrigated. Also, a large part of irrigation depends on the rains, and this year we have had an exceptional drought, unparalleled in the last seventy years. It is a measure of the degree to which the world has become indivisible that in this crisis we have had the full understanding and assistance of many countries and, most notably, of your own. With this support, I have no doubt that we shall tide over the famine without too great a suffering.

We have drawn a long-term and essential lesson from this famine. In agriculture, it is not enough to aim at self-sufficiency. We must produce more. This is the basic objective of the bold new agricultural strategy which has been evolved in India in the last year. This strategy has been based on an intense review for several months preceding the present crisis. Basically, what we are attempting is to break, within a short space of time, the vicious circle of poor incentives, inadequate inputs and low production in Indian agriculture and to achieve a modernized agriculture.

Of equal priority are our plans for population control. Our efforts have received a decisive impetus in the last year or so. Over 18,000 family planning centers are now functioning in the country and we started on an intrauterine contraceptive device program last year. This device, which is simple, inexpensive and harmless, has already become quite popular and on an average there are 100,000 insertions a month. This number is rapidly increasing. In the Third Plan, the expenditure on family planning has been over ten times that spent on the program in the first two Plans put together; more than three times this amount will be allotted for population control in the next five years.

What is important to remember is that, in both agriculture and population control, we have to operate in the diffuse area where success depends on the extent to which individuals accept a change in attitude. At this point, one can truthfully say that the Indian peasant as well as the Indian parent is being rapidly prepared to accept the changed attitude demanded of them by modern society. But ultimately what will convince them to modernize is the example of modernization itself. Nothing succeeds like success, and in the coming years, as examples of progress in India multiply, the pace of progress will certainly accelerate. What is important is that at every stage we should have the resources and the inputs to satisfy this demand for improvement whenever and in whatever form it arises. This then is the challenge for the coming period.

We are at present engaged in the formulation of the Fourth Five Year Plan. It seeks to take India on to a decisively higher stage of development in the next five years. The investment in the Fourth Plan will be $45 billion, nearly twice the investment of around $24 billion in the Third Plan. The strategy underlying this Plan is a rapid reduction in the birth rate, an assurance to the agricultural sector of all the inputs it needs, an emphasis on rapid expansion of exports, and a rapid increase in domestic savings. In drawing up this Plan, we have time and again been impressed by the extent to which agriculture, transport, power and industry are linked together. Fertilizers provide the most obvious example of these links. One of the most important targets is to increase fertilizer production capacity to 2.4 million tons of nitrogen. We already have enough schemes on hand and under active negotiation to ensure realization of this target.

As I see it, India is well past the midpoint of process of development which began in 1951. The next ten or twelve years, of which the Fourth Plan will be only the first milestone, will be a crucial period, as it is within this time span of the next decade or so that India plans to complete her emergence as a fully self-reliant nation. These years will certainly be crucial to the people of India, in terms of the effort and sacrifice which they will be called upon to make. These will also be crucial for our friends elsewhere in the world, in that they will face the test of whether they intend to continue the support which they have given to India so far decisively enough in the future so as to make a difference. The aid which we have received hitherto has been on a generous scale in absolute terms. But, relative to other countries, it has been somewhere at the end of the list on a per capita basis. To some extent this is perhaps due to the enormous size of our country. Nonetheless, the fact remains that unless internal savings are supplemented to an adequate degree by the import of capital, we cannot carry out the very investments which would render the further flow of aid unnecessary in the foreseeable future. I would venture to suggest that from the point of view of the aid-giving countries themselves, it would be far better to render assistance on a scale that promotes early self-generating growth than to run the risk of giving too little. Such a policy would be self-defeating.

This concept of ultimate self-reliance means that aid, which is an extraordinary form of transfer of resources, need not continue and that our own export earnings should meet our import requirements. The flow of private investment would certainly continue; it would be welcome and, indeed, receive greater emphasis. I am aware that most of you in this gathering are keenly interested in our policies in respect of private foreign investment and I shall, therefore, speak quite frankly on this matter. In India, we welcome private foreign investment not only for the capital it brings with it, but also for the transfer of modern technology and managerial and technical skills which it facilitates. In the future, we shall continue to maintain our policy of treating foreign investors completely on par with national investors. Indeed, the foreign investor in India is "discriminated" only in the sense of being allowed certain advantages, such as tax exemption for technicians, which are not available to Indian nationals. Our fiscal structure contains sizable incentives to private investment, Indian and foreign, and these will be continued. We allow full repatriation of profits and capital freely and we intend to continue this policy. Most important of all, India has a large and growing market with a high degree of profitability. In the foreseeable future, it will be one of the world's largest markets, and enterprises established early in the process of development are bound to take a full share in that prosperity. In India, we have a well-laid infrastructure of power and transport. Indian labor has demonstrated that, with proper training and good working conditions, its productivity can compare with that achieved in Western Europe. We have given high importance to technical education and there is no dearth of technicians and engineers in India.

This is the brighter side of the picture. The other side which has been presented to us repeatedly is the existence in the Indian system of a number of controls and allocation procedures which, it is claimed, act as a major inhibiting factor to the smooth flow of private investment. To a large extent, these controls are a product of scarcity. When resources are limited and have to be put to the most productive use within the framework of a system of priorities, it is inevitable that there should be selectivity about the fields in which one wants new investment. To give an obvious example, in the Indian context it would be irrational to assure freedom of investment in cosmetics or similar luxury goods. It is this need for selectivity which necessitates controls.

Having said this, I do fully agree with the plea for a rationalization and simplification of procedures for operating these controls. In this area, wherever the supply situation has improved, such as in steel or cement, we have loosened the allocation procedures. We have also undertaken a number of steps to streamline the approval mechanism. As a major step in this area, I am meeting young Indian industrialists next month to explore with them possibilities for further improvement. Any suggestions which you might like to contribute in this matter individually or in groups are welcome and we shall give them our full consideration.

Ultimately, liberalization of controls is possible only with a greater inflow of foreign resources whether from export earnings or foreign aid or foreign investment. We do not believe in controls for their own sake, and with an additional supply of foreign resources we shall certainly be prepared to relax many of them. On exports we continue to do all we can, but I must point out that the industrialized countries of the Western world need to open up their markets much more than they have been prepared to do so far.

I have outlined our approach to private foreign investment. I feel confident that this approach supplies a framework within which we and you can do business together. In this country you have always believed in pushing back your frontiers. In the last century, you tamed the Wild West. My appeal to you today is that in the next few decades you should allow yourselves to be tamed by the Developing East. In this complex and troubled world of today, the greatest promise for a better future lies in growth in science and technology and in modern means of communication which have brought this world, yours and mine, so close together already. We, in this generation, have the opportunity to use these marvelous tools to secure for the world peace through prosperity. In this quest, India is entirely ready and willing to be your partner.

From address at dinner given by the India Council of the Asia Society and other organizations
[New York, March 31, 1966]

There is little to be said either about India or about Indo-American relations with which you are not already familiar. But, with your permission, I should like to indulge in some loud thinking on matters of common concern.

India and the United States share the values of freedom and peace, religious tolerance and goodwill, care of the weak and the neglected and opportunity for all without sapping the springs of initiative and enterprise. We also share a commitment to political democracy. On us rests a great part of the responsibility of carrying forward, over the coming decades, the traditions of progress with freedom and justice. As the most affluent democracy and the most powerful nation in the world, America has a place in world affairs which is easy to comprehend. India too will be judged by future historians in terms of her success or failures in enriching human dignity and in sustaining freedom among the emerging nations of the world.

There is no parallel in history for what we are trying to achieve in India today. In a vast and ancient land steeped in extreme poverty and embracing within its borders a rich variety of cultures, languages and religions, we are attempting to bridge, in a matter of decades, the gap created by a century and more of stagnation. This we are doing within the framework of an active and highly articulate democracy. For we believe that development can be achieved with consent and with increasing welfare.

The Indian experiment gains meaning and significance in its relevance to two-thirds of humanity for whom the virtues of freedom and of the rule of law have yet to be proven and tested. Neither India nor America can discharge the responsibility which history has bestowed upon them without having a correct perspective of the world in which we live.

Let us look at the world of today. As a result of the manifold initiative already taken towards greater international cooperation, our world is becoming increasingly united. In the second half of the twentieth century, science and technology have definitely tilted the scales in favor of greater hope and promise for all mankind. At the same time, tensions still persist and there is growing inequality between one nation and another. A significant fact is the change in the outlook and quality of the new generation. There is now opportunity for youth to gain recognition, to pursue excellence, and for their talent to flower. In Europe and America, in Asia and Africa, in the Soviet Union and Latin America, the young are restless and are seeking an identity. They are increasingly free from the passions and prejudices of the past. They repudiate the memories and slogans of an age in which wars, depression, colonialism and racial intolerance gave rise to such fierce passions and ideological disputes. Instead, they want to hew their own path of endeavor and self-expression.

In India too the gap between the new generation and the older one is much wider than ever before. Talented young people are emerging in large numbers and from all sections of society. The attitudes of these young people are changing the standard image of India that exists in the minds of most people abroad. Even in the Indian village of today, bound as it is by old custom and tradition, you will find an urge for progress and change. Poverty and want, disease and ignorance are no longer accepted as punishment for past sins. The Indian business community has also come of age. The commercial attitudes of the past are dying and a whole generation of younger businessmen, trained in modern methods of management and attuned to technical and economic efficiency, is emerging to create a new and dynamic industry.

In the political sphere too, we have repeatedly belied the

prophets of gloom. With all our differences and difficulties, India has remained one and united, a secular state where religious tolerance is cherished as much as individual freedom, a federal state where local autonomy is constantly being enlarged without undermining the sense of national unity and purpose.

The question is often asked how, despite all her problems, India has been able to strengthen the foundations of democracy and harmony. The answer is not difficult to find. In Mahatma Gandhi, we had a great leader whose identification with the poorest of the poor gave a strong base to our political party. In my father we had a leader who was young at heart and who retained to the last a fresh and forward-looking mind. He was able to call the nation to great tasks. His leadership was one that stressed self-reliance. He demanded loyalty not to himself but to larger causes. The Congress Party, which Mahatma Gandhi and my father guided, has a tradition of harboring under its canopy a wide range of political opinion. Differences are resolved by debate and discussion

I should not like you to believe—indeed how could I?—that all is well with India or that we do not have formidable problems still ahead of us. With all our progress in the economic field, and it has been considerable, life for the average Indian still retains its harshness. Much remains to be done to bring the benefits of science and technology to our homes, our farms and our factories. Health and education require far greater attention than we have been able to give. In our commerce with other nations, we run an adverse balance which must be met by borrowing from abroad. What should we do to meet this situation? We have initiated a bold new program for raising agricultural production and for encouraging family planning. In regard to external trade also, we are making every effort to increase our export earnings and to produce at home a growing proportion of our rapidly rising needs of fertilizers, pesticides, petroleum products, steel and even machinery. The Indian economy has, over the years, achieved a fairly high degree of sophistication and diversification so that today we are able to manufacture a wide variety of goods and equipment in our own factories.

Some of the difficulties which we are experiencing today in regard to prices, food production and foreign exchange are in large part a reflection of the very success that we have achieved in modernizing and transforming the Indian economy. Progress has brought expectation of even greater advance and the desire to move faster than is immediately feasible. If our economy falters and shows signs of strain, they are difficulties of growth and not of stagnation or incompetence or wrong objectives and policies.

If we had not thought of building the basic industries, we might have moved faster. But there is no escape from setting up basic industry and transport and power. As we grow we have to build the basis of further growth. In President Johnson's words, we must "build for tomorrow in the immediacy of today."

So we continue our endeavor. Four-fifths of our investment of $40 billion in the last fifteen years has come from our own people, mainly through taxation, and mainly from the poor. Only a million Indians are rich enough to pay income tax in a nation of five hundred million people.

The other one-fifth of our investment comes to us as foreign aid. It is a crucial one-fifth, a catalytic one-fifth. It represents new machinery, new technology and the materials needed by our growing industry.

A great deal of our foreign aid comes from the American people. As we draw closer to the turning point, our effort increases and we need a correspondingly greater volume of aid. If this is not forthcoming, the bright tomorrow recedes. As a nation, we do not wish to depend on foreign assistance for a day longer than is absolutely necessary. Our enormous population has made it difficult for us to obtain the kind of external assistance on a per capita basis as has been made available to other, more fortunately placed countries.

With all these disabilities, we do wholeheartedly endorse the principle that foreign aid can be justified only in terms of performance. No nation, not even the United States of America, is rich enough to waste its substance. And no nation, certainly not India, can receive even friendly assistance without paralyzing its will and morale, unless such aid is merely a stepping-stone towards eventual self-reliance.

The assistance we have received so generously from America has been not only on a government-to-government basis. It has also been on a people-to-people and a business-to-business basis. The work of the devoted young people of the Peace Corps, the activities of institutions such as the Ford Foundation and the Rockefeller Foundation, and the presence of a large number of Indian students in your universities—all these are evidence of people-to-people cooperation. As for business, American and Indian businessmen have come closer together in trade and in industry in a number of productive ventures.

I assure those who have a business interest in India or are contemplating such an interest that India welcomes them. We allow repatriation of profits and capital freely. These problems can be discussed frankly with us and need not be raised to the level of international controversy. As a nation, we are hospitable. Investors coming to India will be received as friends. We have no rigid or dogmatic attitudes. Our main concern is the well-being of our people and the viability of our country. Whatever the odds, we must succeed in our experiment of progress with freedom and social justice. Consistent with this, we are prepared to consider any and every proposal for international business cooperation.

The bonds of friendship between India and the United States are strong, but they cannot be meaningful and purposeful without the realization that our two countries have a special responsibility to share at this present juncture of history. To discharge this high responsibility, we must view the present in the perspective of history. We cannot afford to be distracted by impatience or diverted by difficulties or irritated by misunderstandings which seem so inseparable a part of human relations. The quality of statesmanship lies in rising above the vexations and irritations of the day. Nowhere is this quality more essential than in the relationship between India and America.

Address at Columbia University
[New York, November 6, 1971]

Dean Cordier, President McGill, distinguished guests:

I am deeply touched by your words and by your asking me to come here this afternoon. The people of America have always shown an understanding of our problems. During our Independence struggle which has influenced my generation very profoundly and which has shaped our present in India, we took inspiration from the words of some of your own great men. India has strived to stand for freedom and democracy in our own country and in other places because we believe that these qualities, these ideals, are indivisible. We believe that what happens in one part of the world does affect other people and other countries.

Now it is very difficult to know what to say about India even to a distinguished audience such as this who are well-informed, because the country is so diverse, so full of contradictions, that anything you say about it is true of some part and equally untrue of other parts. It is a country of great poverty, but one which is fighting poverty with all its strength. I think that if I were to select just one Indian quality, I would say it is that of tolerance, and I think this is a quality which is so essential for any working real democracy.

The other day in England, I was asked something about the high ideals of India and whether India was a country of high ideals. My reply was that it is true that we have very high ideals, but like other countries India is also inhabited by human beings and not all human beings are able to live up to high ideals. But nevertheless I think it is important if some of us aim at them and try to work our way by difficult, painful steps towards them.

Democracy can have many meanings. The meaning most often given to it in the West is that there should be a two-party system and that people should vote for one party or another. In fact, we were told that because we had many parties, perhaps there was something wanting in our democracy and we should aim at a two-party system. Now frankly to us it seems very strange, because the two parties may not be able to contain all the opinions in a country at a time, though I must admit that sometimes the multiplicity of parties which we have in India is not a very great help to the public. But it is a phase of development, and I do not think it basically affects democracy. We have been able to have democracy, and democracy has been strengthened because of this quality of tolerance, which is an old quality in Indian philosophy and in our way of life.

We have many differences among ourselves. We have differences even within my party, but our method has been to try and talk things over and see how we can minimize the differences or points of dispute, how we can talk and arrive at some kind of working compromise. That is why through the years, even though the people of India are not educated and many of them, I am sorry to say, are still illiterate, it would not be true to say that therefore they do not understand the problems which affect them. We have seen in our elections that every election has been an occasion for the education of people and that they have voted with maturity and understanding. I do not mean to say that many of them are not misled or diverted by irrelevant factors, sometimes by misleading propaganda, but if you will forgive me, I will say that their number is no larger than similar cases in the more educated countries.

The basic problem in India is one of poverty. We feel, therefore, that democracy cannot be real for the people unless it is accompanied by a system which gives greater equality. You all know that the word freedom, the word democracy, did not always mean what they mean today. In periods of history they applied only to a limited group. A few people were privileged people and were known as citizens; the rest may have been slaves or not entitled to the rights of freedom or democracy. But today no one will accept that situation. Today democracy means that every single person living in a country as a citizen should have full and equal rights.

Now this is our attempt in India. Under the Constitution it is so, but in reality it is not really yet. The policy of the Government aims at enabling our people to take advantage of the rights which are theirs under the Constitution. We do not have any dogmatic stand nor do we like to be labeled. Roughly we say we are a secular, socialist democracy. And secular India does not mean antireligion; it merely means that there is no State religion but that all the religions of the different people living there will be equally honored and equally respected. Socialism, we think, is the only way through which we can lessen the disparities between the different sections and, therefore, make democracy more meaningful.

When we were fighting for freedom, we thought freedom was the end, the ultimate aim. But, of course, when we got there, we found it was not. It was merely the opening of a door, the door of opportunity. And the door led to a tremendously difficult path, which was not merely the responsibility of the Government or the party. If we had to go on this journey, we would need the participation and help of all the people of India. Now this is what we are trying to do. We have many parties, parties who are against our basic policies and parties who are not—or at least they say they are not—but say we are not implementing our policies in the manner in which this should be done. We have found room for all these different paths and ideas. And our vision of the future is that it is through cooperation and not conflict that we can go ahead.

Although we have great diversity of language, of religion, even of races, of customs, we do not think it is a weakening factor. In fact, it is a surprise to me when I come abroad and at almost every place I am asked this question, "Will Indian unity hold? How do you manage these different languages?" Well, we have no difficulties at all. Because each State has its language and the people there study in that language. But it does not prevent their working in other States, traveling in other States. It does not upset the basic feeling of Indianness which binds us all together.

Indian unity is an established fact. It is not dependent on a political party or a person. It is something which just exists in India and I do not think that it can easily be diminished or weakened. But there are many tendencies which could weaken unity. In fact, I think in the whole world there is always constant conflict between things that divide and weaken and others which cement together. It is for us to work towards the cementing, uniting, strengthening factors rather than the others.

In the last years since I was in the United States before, India has changed a great deal. We have been through an extremely dark period, a period when the question was asked, "Can democracy survive, can unity survive, can you feed your growing population?" Now we have answered all those questions. Democracy has been strengthened. The last election has proved this if proof were needed. Of course we did not doubt it for an instant. Unity is stronger than ever before, and we are fully self-sufficient in the main cereals which the people eat, that is, wheat and rice. We are now trying to extend our agricultural program to other farm products. We have improved in industry. But there is no doubt that with all this advance, we have merely touched the fringe of the problems which we face. But we face the future with confidence.

Had I come here just a few months ago and you had asked me what are the difficulties, I would have said there are no difficulties now. We are united. We are sure of our direction. And we are going ahead solving our problems one after another. But just a week after our new Parliament met and we were still, in the ways of all democratic societies, congratulating one another on our victory, a terrific new burden fell on us. All of you are aware what it is. So I do not want to dwell on it. But I would like to point to some questions which arise and which we think are very basic questions. We are told today that because our forces and those of West Pakistan are facing each other on the borders, there is a threat of war. And this is true. But the real problem is not because these forces are face to face. The real problem is because of what has happened in East Bengal. If today there is peace in East Bengal, it would not matter if our forces are face to face in the West or in the East. There would be no war. But there is this very serious problem there. And how did it arise? It did not arise because there was insurrection or because there was a desire of one part of Pakistan to separate, to secede, to become independent. No such voice was raised. There was an election held, a free election under the present military leadership of Pakistan. The program for the election was put frankly and openly before the people. If the Government of West Pakistan objected to that program, that was the moment to say, "We will not allow the elections, we cannot allow your six points, we do not approve of them." Nothing was said. The elections were held and the people of both parts of Pakistan overwhelmingly voted for one party—the Awami League.

I am congratulated on my great majority. But it was nothing compared to the majority which Sheikh Mujibur Rahman gained in the election in Pakistan. It was a tremendous victory for him. And he is not an extremist. He was a moderate person. In fact, if I may use the term, he used to be called by some others an American stooge at one time. But once the elections were won, apparently this came as surprise to the Government of West Pakistan and they wanted to find out ways of getting around these results.

Negotiations were begun. We were not in touch with either Sheikh Mujib or his party or East Bengal. We did not know what was happening. We read in the papers that there were negotiations. Later, much later, in fact only about a week before I started on this trip, I happened to meet somebody who said he was present at the negotiations. And on the twenty-fourth of March they thought that they were coming to a settlement, maybe not a satisfactory settlement but still something that could be worked out. But this period was in fact used to bring troops from West Pakistan and on the twenty-fifth of March a reign of terror was let loose. Perhaps you have heard that the biggest concentration, the biggest attack was on the University of Dacca, where a large number of faculty and students were killed on the very first night. Now the entire East Bengali population—the civilians, the paramilitary forces, the East Bengal Regiment and the East Pakistani Rifles—changed their allegiance; that is, they decided to fight the Pakistani Army and that is the base today of the fight of the people of East Bengal. They are the people who are training the guerrillas, young people who are coming across.

Now we are asked the question why is India hesitating to allow United Nations observers? We are not really hesitating because we have some observers already—we have United Nations observers on the Western frontier who have been there since many years and we have about ten people from the United Nations High Commission for Relief of Refugees on the eastern border. Ours is a very open society—anybody who comes, any of you, any of the diplomats who are there, the press, parliamentary delegations from Europe, from Latin America, from Asia, from New Zealand, the Arab countries, the Scandinavian countries, all these people have been to our camps; they have been to the border, and many of them have crossed over and been to East Bengal. Every one of them, without exception, has given one story, which is of the very great misery and the utterly chaotic conditions which exist there. Now in these conditions we are told that there is an attempt to have a civilian government by declaring some seats vacant which are not vacant. The people who were legally, constitutionally elected are still there, but their seats have been declared vacant and I am told that fifty-five people have been declared elected unopposed. Now in the present conditions they can have the whole Parliament declared unopposed because it is surely not possible for anybody to vote.

Now if United Nations observers go, what do they hope to achieve? If they go with the intention of really bringing about peace in East Bengal, they are very welcome on our side: on any side they want to go, we will facilitate their going there. But this is not what they want to do. They want to say what is happening in East Bengal is an internal problem of Pakistan—"we will only want to see what is happening at the border." Now what is happening at the border cannot be divorced from what is happening inside East Bengal. You cannot say, "We will go and try and, well, prevent the guerrillas but not prevent the army killing the people." Well, I cannot even say what is happening to some of the women there. They are not going to interfere with those things, but they do want to interfere with what the freedom fighters are doing.

You may ask, "Is India interfering in this by giving some support?" Well, I can tell you that the people of East Bengal are not very happy with what we are doing for them. They think, and I agree with them, we are doing far too little. And what we are doing is something that we cannot help doing. We cannot stop people going across the border either from the other side to our side or from our side across back to East Pakistan. Had we been able to do this, we would certainly have taken measures to stop these millions of refugees from coming. Because initially the reaction was, well, they are in great trouble, let us allow them in. But very soon the problems that grew for us are really beyond our control and are creating an extremely difficult situation.

The people of America have shown generosity. As I came here, I was given a check. I have been given checks by schoolchildren in different countries, by poor people, all kinds of people, and we are grateful for that help. But the major problem is not a financial one. We are poor, we cannot afford these millions of people. But because we are poor, because we have known how to live without food, without necessities, we can put up with any difficulty. We can look after any number of people, of course with great discomfort to them and to us, and maybe some people will die also. But, nevertheless, we can survive this problem. What is difficult to survive are the political consequences, the social tensions, the difficulty of the administration, and last but most important the real threat to our independence, to our stability, to our integrity. Because with the refugees are coming people who, maybe, are not genuine refugees, we are having sabotage, our trains have been blown up and all kinds of other things.

So India today is facing a real threat. Wherever we have reached in economic growth, in social stability of the people, it hasn't been an easy task; it has been a tremendously difficult task against very great odds. We had help from many countries, including the United States, but it has been a very, very small part of the major endeavor. The major brunt of the problems—whether it is the refugees today or whether it is the problems of our own people—it has been borne by the Indian people themselves. If there is progress, it is because the Indian people have put in the effort, put in the sacrifice that was needed to go ahead.

So just when we come to a stage where we think we can go ahead much more easily, much faster, we suddenly have the problems of another country. They are not our problems. And another country which has pushed across the border those people who did not vote for their Government, for the regime they wanted. There is no other crime which these people have committed because the cry for independence arose after Sheikh Mujib was arrested and not before. He himself, so far as I know, has not asked for independence, even now. But after he was arrested, after there was this tremendous massacre, it was only perhaps understandable that the rest of the people said, "Well, after this how can we live together? We have to be separate."

So this is the situation. We have no animosity towards Pakistan even though they have campaigns—"Crush India, conquer India." I do not know whether the pictures appeared here. But these were the stickers which the population was having. They observed a day or a week and they had these things on their cars. We never had anything like this, and we never shall. We have not had anything against even China. China has attacked us, Pakistan has attacked us. On our side we have always said we want friendship. On our side we have always taken unilateral steps which we thought would lead to a normalization of relations. But there has been no response forthcoming.

Well, we do not mind if there is no response. But we do think that the limit of our endurance has been reached when they think they can just put their troubles onto us. Here was the problem they were facing—that their people had voted against the Government. So what do you do, you send them across the frontier. At one stroke you get rid of your enemies, you get rid of population and you weaken India which you want to weaken. It is something which India just cannot tolerate. Not me; maybe I could tolerate. But with all my majority in Parliament, it is not a dictatorship. I have to carry not only my party, I have to carry in a serious situation all the other parties of India. And we feel that it is not just the question of India, because we believe that if peace is threatened in India, if stability is threatened in India, there cannot be peace and stability in any part of Pakistan. They can have all the armies of the world, whether they have them from China or the U.S.A. or any other country. They cannot bring peace if there is instability in the major part of the subcontinent.

Today by some countries wanting to support the prestige of one man, they are threatening peace in the entire subcontinent. I do not personally think that they can save Pakistan or keep it united or keep it strong by supporting a person who is not an elected person, who is a military dictator. So this is what we are concerned about—not really today's problems but the basic values for which we have fought, for which so many of our people have given their lives. These are the values which are being attacked.

And if they are attacked next door to us, well, what guarantee have we that they can survive in our country and they cannot be attacked there? This is what bothers us. It is not important who is to blame, though I think Pakistan is to blame, but I do not want to score a point in a debate. What is important, how can we now have peace? You cannot have peace just by saying that the troops should move. You can only have peace if the basic problem which has arisen is solved. And the basic problem is not in the West where the troops are facing each other, but in the East.

Since I have mentioned troops, I would like to say one word more, and that is that Pakistan moved its troops about a week or ten days before we did anything. And the United Nations observer who was there took up this question with them. They said, "Well, this is nothing serious, this is just ordinary training exercise." If that reason is accepted, it is very strange indeed that you have these exercises and you keep your troops posted not for a day or two days but over a week. And ten days passed without any action from the United Nations or anybody else. Then we said, well these people may attack, and in order to defend ourselves we must move up our troops. Already twice, or rather three times if you include

China, we have been invaded and found unprepared. No Government can last in a country if the people feel that this Government is not going to defend our country or defend our security.

We waited patiently, hoping that something would be done, some ways would be found. But nobody was bothered. Not a word was said while these troops were on our borders facing us. It was only when our troops went that suddenly the world's concern came up. "Oh, the two troops are facing each other."

It is true that war is a dreadful thing. I have lived through the last war in London, the worst part of the blitz. And I know that now wars are much worse. I know what happens to the civilian population. Never would anybody want war for their people. And certainly India will do nothing to provoke a war or conflict. But India is determined to safeguard her interests. India is determined to keep her freedom intact. India is united as never before, and India feels so strongly about these basic things, whether it is freedom, whether it is democracy. It is a whole way of life with us. It is not a dogma, it is not an ism that we follow. It is a way of life which has kept our nation alive for thirty centuries. And we are not going to have it attacked because it suits somebody or other or does not suit somebody or other. We want help, we want support, we welcome sympathy. But basically in the world every individual ultimately is alone and every nation is ultimately alone. And India is prepared to fight alone for what it thinks worth fighting for.

The fight is not always on the war front. Much of our fight has been a peaceful fight and this is our preference. This is our way, that we should fight and struggle peacefully to establish these ideals. But we are not going to give up the ideals for anything or anybody. We owe a responsibility to our people and to our future generation. We want to bring well-being to our people, but we know that economic progress without social justice has no meaning, and economic progress and social justice without freedom for the people also has no meaning. All these things must go together.

We have learnt a lot from the West but we are determined not to become mere imitators of the West. We want to find our own direction and our own path. We want to find strength in the values which our people have held for all these centuries. Because these values have given us endurance and courage. By Western standards in many things we may be behind and we may be backward, but we have got something in us that has kept us going.

I am asked the question time and again: "How is it that a woman can lead a government or a country?" Do you know this question is never asked in India—not in the smallest village, because our society and our philosophy is based on the importance of the individual. We are not concerned if this person is a man or a woman, if this person is a Christian or a Hindu, or a Muslim. We are only concerned this is a human being, what has he to contribute to society? If he has something to contribute, society should make use of that contribution.

This is what India is trying to do. I do not know whether we will succeed. We can only say that we will put all our strength in taking the country in that direction. We may succeed, we may not succeed. But fortunately our philosophy teaches us that you must do right regardless of whether it brings pleasure or pain, whether it brings success or failure. And we found it, although it seems a very philosophical abstract thought, very practical as well. It is the one thing that really gives satisfaction and ultimately gives success also. And I think that in these years by having a democratic form of government, we may not have achieved the material success that perhaps—I say perhaps because I am not sure that it would have happened—we could have got by, say, a stronger type of government—dictatorship or something like that. But if we have lost in that direction, I think we have gained something by not taking that direction. That gain is in human values, it is in the dignity of the human being. It is the suffering to the individual which has been avoided.

So I think that India has something to offer to the world, but India has also a great deal to take from the world. No country in today's world can live in isolation. Therefore, our policy has been that just as we try to talk and take the people of our country with us no matter how much against us they may be, so with other nations. Today I have a tremendous majority. But on every issue I talk with all the leaders of the Opposition; some of them may have only one representative in Parliament, but still if he or she represents a different point of view, I talk with him or with her. And this is the strength of our democracy and ultimately of our country.

And I think this is the only way that can succeed in the world at large. We each have our way. But we say, what is there in common, what is there that can keep us together and help us to build one world?

I am, of course, very proud of our young people in India because, in spite of enormous difficulties, I think they are facing the challenge of the future, and although sometimes their expression of dissent takes violent forms which I certainly do not approve, I think they are generally groping for something worthwhile, and I hope that by our work we can persuade them to do their groping in a more constructive, cooperative and peaceful way. So I would like to thank you once more for this privilege of allowing me to say a few words to you all and to give you the greetings on my own behalf and on behalf of the people of India. Thank you.

Letter to President Richard M. Nixon
[New Delhi, December 15, 1971]

Dear Mr. President,

I am writing at a moment of deep anguish at the unhappy turn which the relations between our two countries have taken.

I am setting aside all pride, prejudice and passion and trying, as calmly as I can, to analyze once again the origins of the tragedy which is being enacted.

There are moments in history when brooding tragedy and its dark shadows can be lightened by recalling great moments of the past. One such great moment which has inspired millions of people to die for liberty was the Declaration of Independence by the United States of America.

That declaration stated that whenever any form of government becomes destructive of man's inalienable rights to life, liberty and pursuit of happiness, it was the right of the people to alter or abolish it.

All unprejudiced persons objectively surveying the grim events in Bangladesh since March 25 have recognized the revolt of 75 million people, a people who were forced to the conclusion that neither their life, nor their liberty, to say nothing of the possibility of the pursuit of happiness, was available to them.

The world press, radio and television have faithfully recorded the story. The most perceptive of American scholars who are knowledgeable about the affairs of this subcontinent revealed the anatomy of East Bengal's frustrations.

This tragic war, which is continuing, could have been averted if, during the nine months prior to Pakistan's attack on us on December 3, the great leaders of the world had paid some attention to the fact of revolt, tried to see the reality of the situation and searched for a genuine basis for reconciliation.

I wrote letters along these lines. I undertook a tour in quest of peace at a time when it was extremely difficult to leave the country in the hope of presenting to some of the leaders of the world the situation as I saw it. It was heartbreaking to find that while there was sympathy for the poor refugees the disease itself was ignored.

War also could have been avoided if the power, influence and authority of all the states, and above all of the United States, had got Sheikh Mujibur Rahman released. Instead, we were told that a civilian administration was being installed. Everyone knows that this civilian administration was a farce; today the farce has turned into tragedy.

Lip service was paid to the need for a political solution, but not a single worthwhile step was taken to bring this about. Instead, the rulers of West Pakistan went ahead holding farcical elections to seats which had been arbitrarily declared vacant.

There was not even a whisper that anyone from the outside world had tried to have contact with Mujibur Rahman. Our earnest plea that Sheikh Mujibur Rahman should be released, or that, even if he were to be kept under detention, contact with him might be established, was not considered practical on the ground that the U.S. could not urge policies which might lead to the overthrow of President Yahya Khan.

While the United States recognized that Mujib was a core factor in the situation and that unquestionably in the long run Pakistan must acquiesce in the direction of greater autonomy for East Pakistan, arguments were advanced to demonstrate the fragility of the situation and of Yahya Khan's difficulty.

Mr. President, may I ask you in all sincerity: was the release or even secret negotiations with a single human being, namely, Sheikh Mujibur Rahman, more disastrous than the waging of a war?

The fact of the matter is that the rulers of West Pakistan got away with the impression that they could do what they liked because no one, not even the United States, would choose to take a public position that while Pakistan's integrity was certainly sacrosanct, human rights, liberty were no less so and that there was a necessary interconnection between the inviolability of states and the contentment of their people.

Mr. President, despite the continued defiance by the rulers of Pakistan of the most elementary facts of life, we would still have tried our hardest to restrain the mounting pressure, as we had for nine long months, and war could have been prevented had the rulers of Pakistan not launched a massive attack on us by bombing our airfields in Amritsar, Pathankot, Srinagar, Avantipur, Uttarlai, Jodhpur, Ambala and Agra in the broad daylight on December 3, 1971, at a time when I was away in Calcutta, my colleague the Defense Minister, was in Patna and was due to leave further for Bangalore in the South, and another senior colleague of mine, the Finance Minister, was in Bombay.

The fact that this initiative was taken at this particular time of our absence from the capital showed perfidious intentions. In the face of this, could we simply sit back trusting that the rulers of Pakistan or those who were advising them had peaceful, constructive and reasonable intent?

We are asked what we want. We seek nothing for ourselves.

We do not want any territory of what was East Pakistan and now constitutes Bangladesh.

We do not want any territory of West Pakistan. We do want lasting peace with Pakistan. But will Pakistan give up its ceaseless and yet pointless agitation of the last 24 years over Kashmir? Are they willing to give up their hate campaign and posture of perpetual hostility towards India? How many times in the last 24 years have my father and I offered a pact of nonaggression to Pakistan? It is a matter of recorded history that each time such an offer was made Pakistan rejected it out of hand.

We are deeply hurt by the innuendoes and insinuations that it was we who have precipitated the crisis and have in any way thwarted the emergence of solutions. I do not really know who is responsible for this calumny. During my visit to the United States, United Kingdom, France, Germany, Austria and Belgium, the point I emphasized publicly as well as privately was the immediate need for a political settlement.

We waited nine months for it. When Dr. Kissinger came in August 1971, I had emphasized to him the importance of seeking an early political settlement. But we have not received, even to this day, the barest framework of a settlement which would take into account the facts as they are and not as we imagine them to be.

Be that as it may, it is my earnest and sincere hope that with all the knowledge and deep understanding of human affairs you, as President of the United States and reflecting the will, the aspirations and idealism of the great American people, will at least let me know where precisely we have gone wrong before your representatives or spokesmen deal with us with such harshness of language.

With regards and best wishes.

Yours sincerely,
Indira Gandhi

India,
Russia and China

§ INDIA AND
THE UNION OF SOVIET SOCIALIST REPUBLICS

From address at Soviet-Indian Friendship Rally
[Moscow, July 14, 1966]

I have visited this great land many times and my mind is full
of memories, especially of the tour with my father in 1955. The
truly tumultuous welcome we received imparted warmth and
added meaning to the relationship between our two countries.
From the time of the Great October Revolution, the world began
to hear a new voice—that of Lenin—and began to stir to new
ideas. Our own independence struggle in India developed along
somewhat different lines. Nevertheless, we were influenced and
deeply moved by the heroic efforts of the new Soviet Government
to establish itself and build a new social order on the ruins of the
czarist tyranny and war. We were impressed by the foresight and
practical wisdom of your leaders in modifying their tactics and
making adjustments to suit the needs and circumstances of the
time without surrendering their cherished goals. This has been an
example for other countries, as was evident in the deliberations of
your 23rd Party Congress.

The Soviet Seven Year Plan has registered substantial all-round gains. Your splendid successes in probing the unfathomed mysteries of space are but one symbol of your great progress. May I, on behalf of the Indian people, congratulate you, the Soviet people, on this magnificent achievement? We share your pride in the skill and daring of your scientists and cosmonauts, for the conquest of nature is a triumph of all mankind. In a very different sense, we in India too have attained certain objectives which, not many years ago, our people thought unattainable.

In the nineteen years since Independence, there has been a remarkable transformation of the Indian scene. Ten years ago, peasants cultivated their fields around two little villages called Bhilai and Hatia, near Ranchi, as their forefathers had for centuries before them. Today, Bhilai is a mighty steel center and Hatia the hub of a huge machine-building complex. The Soviet Union has helped us in both these projects.

The public sector has taken a leading role in the development of many key industries in India. The past decade has seen a considerable strengthening of the infrastructure. Power and transport facilities have been greatly developed. There has been a tremendous expansion in technical education. A number of social and institutional changes have been effected. Intermediaries on the land have been abolished over large parts of the country and the ownership of land has passed to the tiller of the soil.

A new generation of Indians is rapidly coming to the helm of affairs. These young men and women have grown up in freedom. They have seized the opportunities offered by Independence and have acquired a variety of skills and experience. They have dedication, vision and confidence. Whether workers, technicians, scientists or managers, they are second to none. I am tremendously proud of them and when I see their bright faces during my travels in the country, I am inspired and filled with hope. They are dedicated to the building of a new India, a democratic and socialist India, and they shall succeed in this great adventure.

When we began planning fifteen years ago, it was our objective to end our dependence on foreign aid and attain a stage of self-sustaining growth and a socialist structure of society within the span of a generation. We adhere to this objective and are confident that we shall have developed a self-reliant economy within the next decade, that is, at the end of our Fifth Five Year Plan. With this same end in view, we are proceeding to build a heavy industrial base in the public sector and to develop our exports to a point where we are able to stand on our own feet and repay the foreign loans which we have taken. Just now, we are engaged in giving final shape to our Fourth Five Year Plan.

Some of my colleagues preceded me to Moscow and have had fruitful discussions with your Government on ways and means to promote further trade and economic collaboration between our two countries and peoples. The Bokaro steel plant is a central project in our march towards self-reliance. The Soviet Union is assisting India in building this project and I should like to avail myself of this opportunity to thank Chairman Kosygin and his colleagues for the great interest they have taken in furthering our aspirations with regard to the construction of this project; much of the equipment for this will be assembled from the Soviet-aided machine-building plant near Ranchi to which I have referred earlier. Having now begun to build machines which make machines, we are equally anxious to widen and deepen our own technological design and engineering skill. Here again the Bokaro steel plant will rise as a shining symbol of constructive Indo-Soviet cooperation. India is engrossed in peaceful development. It is engaged in one of the most meaningful and vital struggles of our time—the struggle against poverty.

Everywhere, nations are becoming free, though some dark spots of colonialism and racial oppression still disfigure the map of the world. Yet, political freedom is incomplete and has little meaning without economic independence. Until the battle for economic independence is won, the newly emerging nations—the developing nations—will be subjected to external pressures which must be resisted. The widening gulf between the rich and poor nations is creating new tensions which it must be the object of international economic diplomacy to relieve. In this task, India, though herself in the throes of development, has sought to contribute her mite in assisting other developing nations in Asia and Africa. As our economy develops, so will grow our ability to enlarge our contribution. The world will achieve freedom from want the sooner it is able to secure freedom from war and freedom from fear. That is why India has consistently and from the inception of her Independence stood for nonalignment and peaceful coexistence.

Our entire State policy has been built on the four pillars of socialism, democracy, secularism and nonalignment. We have held fast to these principles and, over the years, have been gratified to see their growing acceptance around the world. There are some who say that nonalignment has served its purpose and has no further role to play. This is a misreading of the international situation. It is the policy of alignment and not of nonalignment which has failed. This is evidenced in the disintegration of SEATO and CENTO. The nature of group tensions might have changed but tensions continue to exist. Nonalignment, cutting across as it does racial and regional barriers and rival power blocs, has got an even more vital role to play in easing these tensions, safeguarding security, strengthening national independence and consolidating peace in our troubled world.

Let us look around Asia and Africa. These are continents newly liberated from colonialism, encompassing a multitude of emerging nations in various stages of social and economic development. One attribute is common to them all. It is nationalism, a sense of national identity, a pride and hope in national aspirations. There are also broader streams of regional nationalism, such as Arab nationalism, which are proud and strong. In the exuberance of their newfound expression, they are assertive, restless. They cannot be ignored. It is hardly surprising that the focus of danger and of international insecurity has moved from Europe to the developing world, the so-called "Third World" of Asia, Africa and Latin America. Here it is that we find the tensions of development and of growth, of nationalist upsurge, of external economic pressure and intrigue, of subversion, of coups, coming to a boil. Here it is that certain powers seek to create and accentuate tensions by calculated attacks on nonalignment and rejection of peaceful coexistence.

India belongs to Asia. And it is of Asia that I should like to speak, and more especially of Southeast Asia. The tragedy of Vietnam has filled us with anguish. War will solve nothing. It can only extend the area of damage and destruction and embitter relations for years ahead. Vietnam is today a powder keg. Any escalation might substantially enlarge and intensify the conflict with grave consequences for the peace of the world. There is no alternative to a peaceful settlement and it is to this end that we must all bend our energies. We in India certainly cannot afford to be bystanders, especially when a part of Asia is ablaze. No power should be allowed to block the path to peace.

It is for this reason that I ventured to give expression to certain ideas on the eve of my departure from Delhi last week. It seems to be almost universally agreed that the best, perhaps the only constructive, course would be to get all the parties concerned—I repeat all the parties concerned—around the negotiating table within the framework of the Geneva Agreement. Meanwhile, there must be an immediate ending to the bombing of North Vietnam. This would create the climate for the holding of a conference and a swift cessation of hostilities and the complete withdrawal of all foreign forces and armed personnel from Vietnam, in full observance of the Geneva Agreement. There is nothing particularly novel in these suggestions. Nor is it our intention to present them in a package, as a rigid formula of any kind. There might be more suitable acceptable alternatives. If so, we would be willing to support such proposals. Our sole objective at this moment is to focus attention on some simple, fundamental propositions and to deny the inevitability of escalation and destruction by the prolongation of the conflict. We have put forward our idea for a conference on Vietnam in the same constructive spirit which prompted you to propose the Tashkent Conference. Peace in Vietnam would also go a long way towards bringing about conditions of greater stability in Southeast Asia which, like most other parts of the world, is in a state of flux.

We are glad that the confrontation between Malaysia and Indonesia is ending and we hope this will lead to widening the area of peace and the strengthening of nonalignment. Our interest in West Asia and Africa is no less keen. The embers of colonialism and racialism might appear to glow in the wind of change. But these are dying embers. In cooperation with other countries we should continue to make all possible efforts to wipe out these remnants of a shameful past.

We support the people of Zimbabwe, South Africa, Angola, Mozambique, so-called "Portuguese" Guinea, Southern Arabia,

Aden and other dependent territories in their struggle for freedom and independence. We consider our own freedom and independence incomplete until all countries under colonial domination achieve freedom. Certain reactionary forces are at work in Asia and Africa. Some of these seek to exploit religion for narrow political advantage. Others are allied to entrenched social and economic privilege. It is not enough to condemn these forces. They can be influenced in positive directions, and it is for the progressive forces to devote themselves to this task.

China and Pakistan are close neighbors of ours. We wish them well and make no claims on either except those of good neighborliness and friendship. We are willing to come to a just and honorable settlement with China at any time. The conflict in which we were involved with Pakistan last year was not of our making. We are grateful to the Soviet Government and especially to Chairman Kosygin for the patience with which they helped to bring about the meeting. India stands committed to the Tashkent Declaration and is willing and anxious to implement it fully, both in letter and in spirit. It was the hope of our late Prime Minister, Shri Shastri, that this would mark a point of departure in Indo-Pakistan relations.

The Tashkent Declaration is a notable document because both parties have agreed to abjure the use of force in the settlement of disputes. The Tashkent Declaration is a manifesto of peaceful coexistence and postulates the pacific settlement of differences between States. We in India bear no ill will towards Pakistan. We remain ever willing to enlarge friendly contacts between our two countries and peoples—through cultural exchange, economic cooperation and collaboration, easing of travel and transit restrictions, and in numerous other ways. I am confident that there is no problem between India and Pakistan which cannot be peacefully settled in a manner consistent with the honor and interest of both countries. We have extended the hand of friendship to Pakistan and hope that they will no longer hesitate to grasp it. We are prepared to meet with Pakistan at any level to discuss our problems and work out just and honorable solutions.

One other issue is of deep concern to us and to all mankind. This is general and complete disarmament. We believe that nonproliferation cannot be an end in itself. It can only be an interim stage which facilitates a movement towards nuclear disarmament. Neither India nor any other country can unilaterally impose a self-denying ordinance on itself if the nuclear powers themselves go on proliferating nuclear weapons and do not come to a rational agreement regarding arms control. It is our hope that discussions on the banning of underground tests will mature into a formal international agreement. Meanwhile, the Moscow Test Ban Treaty is threatened by certain nuclear powers. While some kind of international guarantee to safeguard nonaligned, nonnuclear powers against the threat of a nuclear attack from a nuclear power may be useful, we do not think it is enough. Nor do nuclear-free zones adequately answer the basic problem. These are only first steps. The real answer to nuclear armament is general and complete disarmament. This global problem must be faced without delay.

The United Nations is the main hope of the world. We have always sought to strengthen that body and, despite our differences with China, have continued to support the principle of universality in its membership. We believe also that the United Nations should more truly reflect the present state of the world which has greatly altered since 1945 with the emergence to freedom of a very large number of Asian and African nations. These new nations deserve better representation in the various organs of the United Nations. Our discussions with Chairman Kosygin and his colleagues on all these and many other matters have been frank, friendly and fruitful. For me this visit has been a rich experience—rich not only because of the understanding and wisdom of your leaders, but richer still because of the sincere friendship and desire for peace of the great Soviet people. The people of India rejoice in your success and in your progress. Greetings to the citizens of Moscow. May the spirit of Moscow, the spirit of peace and friendship, always triumph. May the bonds of Indo-Soviet friendship and cooperation grow stronger. May cooperation between our two nations and all other friendly States help consolidate and promote peace in the world. *Bharat-Soviet Maitri Amar Rahe* (Long live Indo-Soviet friendship).

Address over U. S. S. R. television
[Moscow, July 15, 1966]

I bring you India's warmhearted greetings and good wishes. I am grateful to Soviet television for the courtesy of being invited to your homes. I have come several times to the Soviet Union since 1953 and have known Soviet friendship and hospitality. In the name of the Indian people, I should like to thank you personally for the kindness shown to me and to my party.

We are glad to have more and more Soviet visitors in our country—technicians, experts and others. There are also a large number of Indian students and technicians in the Soviet Union. I welcome these people-to-people contacts, for this will strengthen our friendship.

Compared to the Soviet Union, India is much smaller in size but much larger in population. By next year you will have five hundred million Indian friends. India became independent nineteen years ago. We have made tremendous progress in many directions. However, our agriculture still has to keep ahead of population to provide the food and fiber we need. We have taken up many large and small irrigation works, including some giant schemes like the 680-kilometer-long Rajasthan Canal which is converting a sandy desert into a garden and is irrigating the Soviet-aided Suratgarh State Farm. Our food-grains production has increased by 75 percent since 1950 and we hope to be substantially self-sufficient in food grains by 1971.

Before Independence, we had a negligible industrial base. This has grown in size and sophistication. We are today not merely building heavy equipment and machines, but machines which build machines. We have developed and are further expanding a substantial steel industry. Amongst the other articles we manufacture are motorcars, locomotives, ships and aircraft. Within the next decade, we hope to attain a stage of self-reliant growth.

The pace and quality of industrialization in India has been greatly influenced by the generous assistance we have received from the Soviet Union in terms both of plant and equipment and of technical assistance. The most notable examples of Indo-Soviet collaboration are in the field of heavy machine-building, steel, heavy electricals, oil refining and the manufacture of drugs. A second integrated iron and steel works is being established at Bokaro with Soviet assistance. In Delhi, Russian is one of the languages spoken in one of our leading shops and we have an Institute of Russian Studies.

Indo-Soviet trade has expanded very rapidly and the Soviet Union is one of our most important trading partners. The character of this trade has also undergone a change. Whereas previously the Soviet Union used predominantly to export capital goods to India and India raw materials to the Soviet Union, the current pattern of trade reveals a considerable amount of Indian manufactured exports to the Soviet Union—shoes, shirts and knitted garments—and Soviet raw materials and intermediates to India. We place great value on this trade, for experience has taught us that trade on terms of equality and mutual benefit is more valuable than aid.

Socialism is one of the cardinal principles of our State policy, along with democracy, secularism and nonalignment. The attainment of socialism in terms of equality of opportunity, social justice and reasonably comfortable living standards is still a long way off. But we are moving in that direction. The public sector occupies a position of increasing primacy in our economic affairs, especially in key industries. This is increasingly true of trade, foreign as well as internal. The cooperative sector is fast expanding and stimulating the process of socialization of trade.

Alongside, there is the equally important process of social transformation. Agrarian relations have been reformed. There is vast improvement in health conditions. There has been a tremendous boom in education. Women are playing an increasingly active role at all levels of national life. There is an ever-widening pool of skill and talent.

Our foreign policy is based on the principles of nonalignment and peaceful coexistence. These principles are the best safeguards of the independence and integrity of developing nations. Our relations with the Soviet Union and other friendly countries have strengthened nonalignment. This policy is an active not a passive one.

We are deeply concerned with war and human suffering and, at this moment, would like to add our voice to the urgent pleas for a peaceful settlement in Vietnam. Our heart goes out to the courageous people of Vietnam. They must be left free to decide their own destiny without interference from outside forces or pressures. The bombing of North Vietnam must stop and peace talks should be held to facilitate the cessation of all hostilities, withdrawal of all foreign armed personnel, and a political solution.

We are grateful to the Soviet Union for helping bring about the Tashkent Declaration between India and Pakistan. India fully supports this declaration and is anxious to implement it. Our position on racialism and colonialism, our desire to see complete disarmament, and our concern to narrow the dangerously widening gulf between rich and poor nations are well known.

On these problems and others, the Soviet Union and India have been and are in a large measure of agreement. I have had useful discussions with Chairman Kosygin and his colleagues. I shall carry back with me to India the warm glow of Indo-Soviet friendship. I know that we have a good friend in the Soviet Union and I shall like you, the Soviet people, to know that you have no less a friend in the Indian people. This friendship is not merely a fact. It is an important factor in international relations.

I wish the Soviet Government and the friendly Soviet people success in their endeavors for further progress at home and peace in the world. *Dosvidanya!*

Address at dinner given for Chairman Aleksei N. Kosygin of the Council of Ministers of the Union of Soviet Socialist Republics
[New Delhi, January 25, 1968

It is a long-awaited pleasure to have our good friend, Chairman Kosygin, and his charming daughter, Mrs. Ludmila Gvishiani, with us. We are happy to welcome you, Chairman Kosygin, on this festive occasion. Our Republic Day celebrations will be the more joyous for the presence in our midst of good friends and neighbors. We regret that you cannot stay longer to see more of the immense variety of our country.

I recall our delightful meeting, only a few months ago, when

Chairman Kosygin took time off from his many pressing engagements at the time of the 50th Anniversary celebrations of the Great October Revolution to invite us, together with some of his distinguished colleagues, to a quiet, informal evening at his dacha outside Moscow. The talk touched many subjects but most memorable was the openhearted friendship and sincerity which underlay it.

Thirty-seven years ago, on this day, the people of India took a pledge not to rest until they became free. Now it is eighteen years since we became a Republic, an event the anniversary of which we are celebrating tomorrow. In these eighteen years, our experience has proved that freedom is only the beginning; its fulfillment is the happiness of the people and their ability to live without fear. But the technology of war has developed to such an extent that a great question mark seems to be poised over the globe. Is man born to blow himself up and destroy his planet? Can he not endure and build? The very nature of modern war has strengthened the compulsions for survival. I recently came across a profound thought in one of our ancient books, to the effect that "when we believe, we perceive." If we believe in the future of man, we shall be able to perceive and strengthen those forces which will help us to realize this belief.

Mankind is one, but people belong to different backgrounds. They are at differing stages of historical evolution and they hold diverse political beliefs. This diversity is essential for the very existence of the world. Attempts to impose doctrines of uniformity have not only failed but have proved to be a danger to peace. Our policies are based on an appreciation of this truth. Coexistence, although regarded by some as a truism, is still the only possible basis for international relations. It is rooted in present-day realities, and provides the framework for the survival of the human race.

The developing friendship between the Soviet Union and India is a good example of international cooperation. It has been of mutual benefit and it has helped freedom and peace.

We have worked together for these great objectives, and you have helped us in working for another equally worthy endeavor—the fight against backwardness. Economic cooperation forms a valued part of the growing Indo-Soviet friendship. In all parts of this

vast land there are visible and living monuments to this cooperation and friendship.

The pattern of this economic cooperation—consisting of
credits, material and technical assistance and increasing stress on
trade—has pioneered a new trend in international economic relations. We are confident that, with the help we are receiving and
even more through our own unremitting effort, we shall win notable victories in our struggle against backwardness.

The past two years have been most difficult for us. They have
been years of extraordinary drought and economic hardship. This
year we have had an excellent harvest; although the months to
come will not be easy, we can look ahead with hope and confidence. Our economy is in transition. We have come up against
problems of economic management, organization and administration. These have served to emphasize that development has more to
it than mere investment.

I lay stress on our economic ties, because for a country like
India development and the struggle against poverty is the central
problem. Our political independence will not be complete or secure until we are economically self-reliant. Our faith in planning is
based on the belief that this is the only way for us to ensure a better life for our people and to narrow the disparities within our society. We are especially anxious to do our best for our children and
young people. All who have visited the U.S.S.R. have come to ad-
mire the great solicitude with which the Soviet Government sur-
rounds its children and youth. I was specially impressed with the
part which the Young Pioneers took in the celebrations of the 50th
Anniversary. They added color and warmth to the functions.

In a few days, the second United Nations Conference on Trade
and Development will take place in Delhi. We attach high importance to this conference, for we believe that the widening disparity
between the rich and the poor, the favored and the underprivileged, threatens the peace of the world as much as it militates
against social justice. The Socialist States represent a large and
powerful economic force. They can make significant contribution
towards the success of the second UNCTAD.

Poverty and economic disparities are not the only threats to
peace. Vietnam—indeed the entire Indo-China peninsula—and

West Asia show how near the brink we find ourselves. The year has just begun. It is too early to say whether it will see a lessening of the tensions and fears which it has inherited. Every time there is some little hope of a turn towards peace, it is soon frustrated. It should be the duty of all who are interested in the cause of peace and humanity to prevent any aggravation of the conflict and to press for a stoppage of bombing as an essential preliminary to negotiation. In West Asia, we trust that the patient efforts of the United Nations will open the door to a just and honorable settlement. We hope that 1968 will be a year of peace and progress and that the pressure of progressive world opinion will help to eliminate the remnants of colonialism and racialism in southern Africa.

We in India have unfortunately had conflicts forced upon us. With you in our midst, Mr. Chairman, our thoughts inevitably turn to the historic Tashkent Declaration, of which you were the prime architect. That declaration charted a path to cooperation and understanding on the basis of peaceful coexistence and good neighborliness. India is ready and willing to tread that path. We should like to have normalization of relations with Pakistan to pave the way for friendship and cooperation. But their cooperation in this task is equally essential. We have a saying that we cannot clap with one hand.

India firmly adheres to the principles of peaceful coexistence and nonalignment which, together with democracy and socialism, constitute the essential pillars of our policy. We shall not swerve from these basic ideals which we interpret in terms which are dynamic and consistent with the changing circumstances, yet without prejudice to the real spirit which underlies them.

May I once again express our pleasure in having you, Chairman Kosygin, and other members of your party with us? I hope that you and your daughter will have an interesting and enjoyable stay in our country.

§ INDIA AND THE PEOPLE'S REPUBLIC OF CHINA

From address at reception
[New York, April 1, 1966]

A question that may be asked is, if China threatened India, then what is India doing to combat Peking's designs in Southeast Asia? China is taking great care to avoid direct military involvement in Vietnam. But China's shadow does fall across Southeast Asia. The real threat from China, however, is less military than political and economic. The Chinese influence will be diminished if its neighbors in Asia and the nations of the developing world can build up popular and forward-looking nationalist governments dedicated to fulfilling the aspirations of their people. They would also be greatly strengthened in this purpose were they to see a strong and viable alternative model. It is precisely by a successful effort to develop democracy that India can answer the Chinese challenge.

India is part of that rural countryside that the Chinese leaders would win and use in their revolutionary approach on the advanced industrialized cities of the West. It is in this large and populous rural countryside that the Chinese influence can and must be stemmed. India is fighting this battle through its devotion to the democratic ideals, through perseverance in planned development and its struggle against poverty. India is militarily holding a two-thousand-miles-long Himalayan frontier against China. India is also fighting this battle in the crucial forum of Afro-Asia which China has sought to use as a political launching pad and as a revolutionary substitute for the United Nations. India's contribution in this regard has earned little notice or thanks. But, I venture to suggest that this is a contribution of high significance, since it has the unique distinction of meeting China's challenge on the ground and plane of Peking's own choosing.

From address in Parliament
[New Delhi, December 22, 1967]

China continues to maintain an attitude of hostility towards us and, as Honorable Members know, spares no opportunity to malign us and to carry on anti-Indian propaganda not only against the Indian Government but against the whole way of our democratic functioning and even our national integrity. But I would like to say that we do not harbor any evil intention towards the Chinese people, and we do hope that a day will come when they will also realize that it is in the interest of all the countries of Southeast Asia that we should be friends and that each country should be able to devote its strength to solving the very major problem of combating poverty and backwardness.

India,
Nonalignment and the Third World

§ INDIA AND THE SOCIALIST FEDERAL REPUBLIC OF YUGOSLAVIA

Address at dinner given by President Josip Broz Tito
[Brioni, July 10, 1966]

Your words, Mr. President, bring to mind memories of a great friendship between you and my father, both partisans of peace, and the larger friendship it symbolized between the people of Yugoslavia and India. Your thoughts reflect the feelings of my own country and people. Your people and mine share similar hopes and aspirations.

The courageous people of Yugoslavia have always stood and struggled for freedom and are fulfilling their aspirations under your determined and dynamic leadership. These aspirations include not only the reassertion of the national personality but the realization of a social and economic revolution ensuring equality, progress and prosperity. Your bold and far-reaching experiments in the social and economic spheres have aroused worldwide interest and are of immense value to us in India.

Mr. President, you have referred to the historic meeting here ten years ago between my father and yourself together with our mutual friend, President Nasser. I am glad that India will have the honor and pleasure to welcome you and President Nasser in October this year. This will be a meeting of three friendly and like-minded countries who are dedicated to the concept of nonalignment as an instrument of peace and peaceful coexistence. It will be a revival of the practice of holding periodic meetings between our three friendly Governments. It is only natural that such discussions should be held from time to time to take stock of our common problems and to coordinate and collaborate our efforts in pursuance of our common objectives.

Mr. President, the dangers of the cold war and armed intervention are no less today than they were eleven years ago. Although some problems have been solved, new tensions have developed. The principle of nonalignment has as much validity today as it had when it was first conceived.

When the world has become one neighborhood, Vietnam is no longer a faraway country. The suffering of the people of Vietnam is the world's peril. That is why on the eve of my departure I gave expression to some ideas on this problem. We cannot be the silent and helpless spectators of a situation which entails so much human suffering to the people of Vietnam. Peace is not the concern of great powers only, but of vital interest to all mankind. A special responsibility devolves on the nonaligned countries, as indeed upon all countries, to find ways and means of a just solution which meets the legitimate rights and hopes of the people of Vietnam. There is no alternative to a peaceful solution, except a bitter and bloody war that could engulf the entire world.

Mr. President, we must build a better world, a more prosperous world. We must give greater social and economic content to nonalignment and coexistence, for how can there be a stable and peaceful coexistence between affluence and poverty, between very rich and very poor nations? Colonialism is dying but its ghost will haunt the world until political independence is matched with economic viability. Nonaligned nations have a positive and a creative role in promoting economic development and social change, and in protecting developing nations from external pressures.

More and more nations are today subscribing to nonalignment while military alliances are steadily weakening. Ten years ago nonalignment did arouse suspicions in certain quarters. Today, it is accepted and respected as an area of peace and disengagement, a bridge between conflicting blocs, an instrument for reducing world tensions. The world is not yet free from the threat of nuclear annihilation. Proliferation of nuclear arms constitutes a real danger. We have a responsibility to urge and assist general and complete disarmament.

Our two countries differ in size and historical background, yet our problems are similar. We are composite societies comprising diverse ethnic and linguistic groups. We are both developing nations. We are both on the path of socialism, though Yugoslavia is far more advanced along the road than we are. We are both convinced that the tasks of economic transformation and social justice demand two prerequisites, peace and international cooperation. Sharing so much in common, it is but natural that India and Yugoslavia should draw closer together. I welcome your words, Mr. President; I too should like to see cooperation between our two countries grow, and grow more rapidly in every field—in trade, industrial development, exchange of technical personnel and other fields. I also attach a value to greater contacts between the younger generation through our universities and research establishments.

Our ties are close. Our friendship is firm. May our friendship grow stronger and our relations closer.

From address at dinner given by
President Josip Broz Tito
[Belgrade, October 11, 1967]

Your words have touched me deeply. To come to Yugoslavia and to meet you and Madame Broz is certainly a privilege; even more so is to find understanding hearts and the warm and strong handclasp of true friendship.

You were kind enough to talk of the closest cooperation and mutual understanding which have characterized the relations between our two countries for a number of years. This is reflected in the continuous exchange of visits between our countries at all levels.

I myself was last in your country on the beautiful island of Brioni in July 1966 and had very cordial and fruitful talks with you and your colleagues. Some months later, we were privileged to welcome you and Madame Broz in India, and we also had the opportunity of holding a tripartite meeting with our mutual and esteemed friend, President Nasser. Recently, we had the privilege of receiving your Foreign Minister, Mr. Nikozic; and our Foreign Minister also paid a visit to you. I mention these not as a bare recital of visits but as evidence of our will to work together in political and economic fields in order to extend the boundaries of mutual cooperation and to concert our action in defense of peace.

Today, world peace hangs by a slender thread. While there is some movement towards a nonproliferation treaty, the nuclear arms race continues to loom large on our horizon. This is bad enough. What is worse is that racialism and colonialism continue to divide and oppress people in new forms. In such a situation, it is the duty of all men and nations of goodwill to unite and throw their weight behind the forces of peace by unceasing exploration of all avenues of cooperation and in the interest of a just and honorable settlement of disputes through peaceful means.

You have referred to the continuance of the deep tension and unresolved crisis in West Asia. This continued stalemate is a threat to peace. Aggression must be vacated. Only on this basis can the problem of security of nations in this region begin to be tackled. Other problems, economic as well as human, can be considered separately. We have followed with keen interest the great efforts which you have made in personally visiting a number of Arab capitals and in sending special envoys to other capitals of Europe and Latin America. Our good wishes and hopes accompanied you on your journey. As a result of these sincere probings, there emerged a series of constructive ideas which have provided the modus vivendi and which contain the basis for a lasting settlement. We have welcomed and supported your initiative as also your ideas and shall continue to do so. Through this period it has been useful to have the closest contact with you and your representatives and to share the information. Many difficulties are yet to be overcome, but we can discern a wider recognition of the need for finding a political solution of the West Asian crisis. We must continue to pursue our efforts to make this possible.

We are glad that, in this hour of great national crisis, our friend and colleague, President Nasser, weathered the storm with great wisdom and courage. We sent him our message of solidarity. I am firmly convinced that the great historical movement of the Arab people will go forward in strength and unity towards the achievement of its progressive aims. The tide of Arab nationalism cannot be reversed. Statesmanship consists in recognizing the validity as well as the vitality of this great movement of the Arab people towards national self-expression.

Mr. President, you have also referred to the long, bitter, cruel and unnecessary war which continues to play havoc with the lives of the Vietnamese people. But there can be no end to the conflict except by political means, on the basis of acceptance of the right of the Vietnamese people to decide their own destiny. When we make suggestions for ending the Vietnam conflict, we should like it to be clearly understood that our purpose is not partisan unless passionate devotion to peace is regarded as partisanship.

Tripartite discussions between our two countries and the U.A.R. have established the groundwork on which, I hope, we shall be able to build a worthy edifice of economic and technical cooperation. Our interest in this interregional economic partnership is not incompatible with our interest in fostering intraregional cooperation with our Asian neighbors.

Our two countries are firmly linked by the bonds of sincere friendship which is based on shared ideals and purposes. We deeply cherish our relations with Yugoslavia and are confident that they are contributing to peace, understanding and progress in the world.

§ INDIA AND THE UNITED ARAB REPUBLIC

Address at reception for President Gamal Abdel Nasser
[New Delhi, October 10, 1966]

Your excellency, I have great pleasure in welcoming you here. You have been with us on several occasions, and each one of your visits has left us a little happier and stronger and more keenly aware of your love and friendship for us. In the world today, our two countries are facing similar difficulties. As you said in your speech, freedom does not merely mean political independence; to be complete and meaningful, it has to include economic strength and self-reliance. To improve our economic condition and take the country forward on the path to prosperity, the Government and people of India are engaged in a supreme effort. Your country is also engaged in a similar effort. It is strange that whatever advance has been made in the fields of science and technology seems to benefit those who are already advanced more than those who are not so advanced. The richer nations are becoming richer. This should be a matter of concern to you and to us and to all the other newly independent and developing nations of the world.

It is this problem which has brought the leaders of the three friendly nations—India, U.A.R. and Yugoslavia—together here to consider the means of cooperation through which we could strengthen our voice in the assemblies of the world. We do not want this merely to enable us to get help from others, but mainly to be able to help one another. This was the main objective of the Tripartite Meeting. Our three countries have chosen a common path of cooperation. I do not know how many more countries will be willing to take to this path. It is very much our wish to take along with us as many as possible of the newly independent countries who are facing the kind of problems that we are facing.

In the past, freedom struggle in one country has provided inspiration and strength to similar struggles in other countries. Those who led the freedom struggle in India were fully aware of the fact that our own freedom could not be secured so long as freedom of any other nation was in peril. Today, a conflict in one part of the world becomes a danger to our own peace. Similarly, social or economic backwardness in any part of the world poses a threat to our freedom and progress.

In our country we are making a special effort to raise those sections of our society that have been neglected in the past. The same principle should be extended to the world community. Peoples or countries neglected in the past are deserving of special assistance. This is necessary to enable all sections of humanity to share equally in the gains made in the fields of science and technology. Development is a common task. Success in this task is possible only when all the countries cooperate. Some advance is possible by one's own effort; but this effort needs to be strengthened by assistance and support from those engaged in a similar effort of their own.

Your visit to this country has made our friendship stronger. With the further growth of this relationship, we should be able to attract other countries of the world also into its fold.

Today, the progress in the field of communication has made it possible for people in one part of the world to reach another part of the world within hours. It is remarkable that the relationship between our two countries dates back to the time when the means of communication were not so advanced. There was even then trade between us and also exchange of ideas. It is a matter for gratification to us that each passing year brings new strength to our old relationship. I welcome you once again not only on behalf of this city, or the Government of India, but also on behalf of the entire Indian People.

§ INDIA AND THE THIRD WORLD

Address at the Third Conference of the Heads of State or Government of Nonaligned Countries
[Lusaka, September 1970]

I welcome this opportunity to give the greetings of the people of India to the government and people of Zambia and to the heads and representatives of the nations who have gathered here. We must also thank President Tito. But for his efforts this meeting would not have taken place. We are glad that this nonaligned conference is meeting for the first time in southern Africa, close to the spirit, the mood and the very heartbeat of Africa.

Here in Lusaka, we can feel the ebb and flow of the continuing battle against remnants of colonialism in Angola and Mozambique. We can feel the vibrations of the struggle against the minority government in Zimbabwe, against the apartheid policies of the racist regime in the Union of South Africa and the national movements in Namibia and in Guinea Bissau. These freedom fighters are engaged in the same battle as we were only recently. They are risking their lives for the same principles that we hold dear. All of us who are meeting here extend our support to these brave men and women.

As I said yesterday, the revolution of our times is unfinished, and the purpose of this conference is to formulate a clear program of action to carry it forward. This is the challenge that the decade of the seventies places before the nonaligned countries.

Only a short while ago, the issues of war and peace, of the disposal of human beings and their destinies, were decided in a few capitals of the world. No longer is it so. Because millions of people in the resurgent continents of Asia, of Africa, of Latin America and the Caribbean have come into their own. Because we determined that decisions involving us—whether concerning war and peace or the direction and pace of our social, economic and political development—could be made only by us, in our own way, and in our own countries. That is how nonalignment was born. It expressed our individual and collective sovereignty, our devotion to freedom and peace and our urgent need to give a better life to our people and the opportunity to live in freedom, in dignity and in peace. At no time was there any intention to set up a third world.

This is our endeavor. The odds are tremendous. Each step has met with criticism and opposition. But we have carried on. Let us not be deterred by cynics and the hostile propaganda of the powerful media of communications. From the beginning, there has been no lack of inquisitors who looked upon nonalignment as heresy, and distorted its meaning. They said it would not work. And yet,

can we not answer back today in the famous words of Galileo—
"And yet, it moves!"

The criticism of nonalignment has shifted on two counts.
Those who now concede that nonalignment had some utility in the
days of the cold war confrontation maintain that this is no longer
so. The reviling is not any more about the basis and principle, but
of its practice.

Have the nonaligned states lost their relevance? The answer is
an emphatic no. Twenty-five years after the last holocaust, the
world is not yet on the brink of peace. The nuclear balance of terror still confronts us. The war in Vietnam is said to be waged with
"conventional" weapons, yet these include chemical contamination
of food and plant life. The only way to have a clean war is not to
have a war at all. Hence India stands and works for total disarmament.

The great powers certainly have the major responsibility for international peace and security. We welcome all initiatives towards
the resolution of differences through negotiations, but even if they
reach accord on their common interests and decide upon mutually
acceptable limitation of strategic arsenals, the rest of the world, of
which we form a considerable part, could hardly remain mere on-
lookers. We have an equal stake in peace, but the quality of this
peace should be such as will ensure our own sovereignty and security.

Not only national honor but national interest demand that we
do not mortgage our decisions in domestic and in international affairs to any foreign dictate. This was one element of our policy of
nonalignment. As the logical corollary, we rejected the enmities of
our erstwhile rulers. We cultivated relations with all countries. As
my father declared: "We are in no camp and in no military alli-
ance. The only camp we should like to be in is the camp of peace
which should include as many countries as possible."

I am grateful to this conference for the gracious gesture in
memory of my father and to the many distinguished delegates who
made references to him.

We decided that our respective territories should not be used
for the subjugation of other people, for subversion or for the carv-
ing out of spheres of influence. Indian manpower and resources had

been used for imperialist purposes. Once free, we declared that this would no longer be permitted.

Subjected to domination, exploitation and the humiliation of racial discrimination as we all had been, how could we compromise with racialism in any form? The pernicious theory that one man is superior to another merely on the ground of race or birth has been proved to be false, yet it continues to dominate the thinking of many.

We believe that today's world is a single entity. We are deeply convinced that by staying out of military pacts the nonaligned countries can use their collective wisdom and influence to tip the balance of power in favor of peace and international cooperation.

These have been the positive achievements of nonalignment. If today there is a weakening of the belief in the efficacy of military pacts, if historic animosities are giving way to essays in friendship and cooperation, if a breadth of realism is influencing international policies towards detente, the nations assembled here can claim some credit. However, this should not lull us into complacency, but encourage us to persevere.

The big powers have never accepted the validity of nonalignment. Neither colonialism nor racialism have vanished. The old comes back in new guise. There are subtle intrigues to undermine our self-confidence and to sow dissensions and mutual distrust among us. Powerful vested interests, domestic and foreign, are combining to erect new structures of neocolonialism. These dangers can be combated by our being united in our adherence to the basic tenets of nonalignment.

I have touched upon certain general points but, on such an occasion, one cannot ignore some of the explosive situations which confront the world.

I should like to take this opportunity to convey our admiration and best wishes to President Gamal Abdel Nasser for his statesmanship and courage in accepting the cease-fire. We disapprove of Israel's intransigence. Israel should be prevailed upon to comply fully with the United Nations Security Council resolution of November 1967. We cannot ignore the inalienable right of the people of Palestine to the homelands from which they were exiled.

The situation in Southeast Asia has further deteriorated. We are deeply concerned about the spreading of the conflict to Cambodia. All foreign forces should withdraw from the various countries of Indochina, the lead being given by the United States. Our assessment, based on talks with the various parties concerned, has led us to believe that a broad-based government, comprising all elements of South Vietnam, would pave the way for the success of the Paris talks. Recent developments in Laos indicate the possibility of talks between the two sides there. As a member and chairman of the International Commission, we have offered our good offices to both the concerned parties for this purpose. To preserve peace and to provide for the reconstruction of this war-torn area, some kind of international convention or agreement should be signed by all the parties concerned as well as the great powers and other interested parties to ensure respect for the neutrality, independence, territorial integrity and sovereignty of all the Indochina states.

We have been deeply disturbed by the reported intention of the United Kingdom and other governments to supply arms to the government of South Africa. This dangerous and retrograde step will threaten the neighbors of South Africa and also the Indian Ocean area. Any accretion to South Africa's military capability will abet its policy of apartheid and racial discrimination, and may encourage it to annex other territories. The argument that this is being done to protect the so-called security of sea routes is untenable. We would like the Indian Ocean to be an area of peace and cooperation. Military bases of outside powers will create tension and great power rivalry.

The spirit of freedom goes hand in hand with the spirit of equality. Beyond the political problems of the unfinished revolution, there are complex and difficult economic tasks. However, a realistic appraisal of our natural resources, our capacities and our competence reveals the possibility for us to work together to reduce our dependence on those who do not respect our sovereignty so that economic leverage for thinly disguised political purposes cannot be used against us. Neocolonialism has no sympathy with our efforts to achieve self-reliance. It seeks to perpetuate our position of disadvantage. International markets are so manipulated in such a way that primary producing countries have a permanent handicap. The levers of technology are also operated against us through unequal collaboration and royalty agreements.

Hence we have to redouble our effort to gain for each nation the opportunity to develop to its full stature. The primary responsibility rests upon each developing country. But we also owe a duty to one another. The fallacy that there is no complementarity between our economies has so far made it difficult to realize the undoubted potential of mutual cooperation. There is greater complementarity among our economies than between the economies of developed nations. Yet advanced nations have been more successful in forging instruments of cooperation among themselves and our own effort in this direction has not even begun. The potential of trade and economic cooperation among us has been left virtually unexplored. By meeting each other's needs, we would diversify our trade, safeguard it against the caprices of international commerce and reduce our dependence on middlemen and brokers.

This conference should formulate the manner in which we could strengthen one another, and give due priority in our national policies to positive measures for mutual cooperation. Such cooperation will help each of us to find some solutions to our respective problems and also give us the capability to induce these changes in the economic system at the global level.

Through the United Nations Conference on Trade and Development, we have tried to persuade the international community to make the changes which have been overdue in the economic system. This is now well understood all over the world. Yet only some have been accepted in principle and even their implementation has been tardy. In a few weeks the second development decade will be launched by the United Nations General Assembly. So far there has been little progress in evolving the guidelines for international cooperation. Many nations which have the capacity, and if I may say so, the duty to make a decisive contribution, hedge their statements with reservation. For too long has international cooperation been viewed as a one-way traffic from the rich to the poor nations.

As the Prime Minister of Guyana said yesterday, between ourselves we possess the major part of the world's natural resources. Our manpower resources are no less plentiful. It should not be beyond our ingenuity to develop these resources and employ the manpower for the production of wealth for our peoples. Because of historical circumstances, economic relations have not been developed among ourselves, but between each of our countries and the erstwhile metropolitan powers. We can now make the first attempts to discover areas of cooperation in many fields of development, generation of power, development of agriculture, improvement of roadways, railways and telecommunications, the expansion of higher education and training in science and technology. If we decide—and I hope we shall—to make a beginning with this study, India will be glad to play its modest part.

We all recognize the malaise afflicting the development process. We know of the growing gap between developed and developing countries, between the northern and southern hemispheres, of the indifference of the affluent, the disappointments of the first development decade, the failure of the affluent countries to transfer even one percent of their gross national product. We are painfully familiar with the pitfalls of "aid," in which the bulk of credits are tied to purchases from donor countries and with the fact that a big portion of new credits goes to the repayment of old loans. But the question is: Must we endlessly wait in the hope that someday the developed countries will undergo a change of heart and realize that disparities in the world are not in their own interest? I am not a pessimist, but I think we should not expect miracles of magnanimity. Even if this should happen I am afraid that it would be of no avail in the absence of the right conditions in our countries. We must determine to help ourselves, to sacrifice, to pool our resources of knowledge and initiative. We must work together on a bilateral, regional and multilateral basis.

From my own experience, I know that willpower, consistent endeavor and the capacity for sacrifice sustained and strengthened us during our struggle for political independence. These same qualities will help us towards economic freedom.

The power to question is the basis of all human progress. We are free because we question the right of others to rule over us. But intellectual and cultural emancipation is just beginning. We are rediscovering ourselves and the fact that a country sees things in terms of its own geography and history. Those who dominated the world's political affairs and manned its economic controls also imposed a monopoly of ideas. For years we accepted their values, their image of the world and strangely enough even of ourselves. Whether we like it or not, we have been pushed into postures of imitation. We have now to break away from borrowed models of development and evolve models of the worthwhile life which are more relevant to our conditions—not necessarily as a group but as individual countries with their distinctive personalities.

The world today is united in peril, not merely the peril from nuclear destruction but the more insidious daily pollution of our environment. It should be united in prosperity and in the blossoming of the spirit of man. The nonaligned countries must be in the vanguard of the movement to create the world of tomorrow and to enrich the content of human life.

The unfinished revolution can reach fulfillment if we have faith and confidence in ourselves and the assurance that however long and arduous the journey ahead we shall reach our destination.

part 3
REMEMBERING THE GREAT

§ RABINDRANATH TAGORE

From address in Parliament
[New Delhi, July 31, 1966]

Shri Samar Guha talked of Gurudev Tagore being a *mahakavi*
[great poet]. He was certainly a *mahakavi*. But he was something
much bigger than that. Poetry was only one part of him. He was a
very great human being and it was our great privilege to have him
as a fellow Indian. But I do not think it would be right for us to
claim that he belonged only to India. He had great influence all
over the world. He was a symbol of what we regard as Indian culture and of the values which have come down to us through the
ages. In fact, I think, although many other great Indians have also
supported these values and have put them into modern language to
make them more comprehensible to the ordinary man, it was
Gurudev who was able to give the clearest articulation and the
greatest cohesion to them.

All of Gurudev's ideas, poems and prayers were concerned not
with any narrow culture but with, for instance, freedom—freedom
not merely in the political sense but freedom from ignorance,
freedom from superstition, freedom from bigotry and narrowness.
All his ideas and attempts were to lift the human being to a higher
level. A fact to remember is that nobody has ever been able to
suppress for long the ideals of freedom and justice and the ideals
for which Gurudev stood.

I do not think that Gurudev needs tribute or homage from us,
because that homage exists in the hearts of the people; it is some-

145

thing which is not just for a few generations but will remain with us for all time to come. Tagore is now a part of our culture, a part of our rich heritage; not only of our own heritage but, if I may say so, of the heritage of the world. He is one of those Indians who established links with the rest of the world. He stood for the widening of the human vision and, if I may use a rather unpoetic word, the cross-fertilization of cultures and ideas. Along with that, he was deeply conscious of the condition of the Indian people. He always identified himself with what he, in one of his beautiful poems, calls the "lowliest and the lost." He talked of high ideals and beauty, and yet he was ever conscious of the need to work for the poorest and those who had been oppressed in our country and elsewhere.

From Convocation Address at Visva-Bharati University
[Santiniketan, December 24, 1967]

Nothing in the world is entirely new and nothing in the world is changeless. Life is a continuous process of adjustment. This is evident at Santiniketan. It is certainly growing and changing, and yet it retains a quality of gentleness, as if the beneficent spirit of Gurudev Tagore was still present. Gurudev was himself part of all time. He conversed with the sages of the dawn of our civilization, yet he walked in the modern age. He combined the eternal and the immediate. He reconciled the universal with the local. That is why he gave the name Visva-Bharati to this great school. He wanted every student of this university to become a *visva-manava,* a universal individual, who knew no narrowness and who could say, "The world is my home and all men are my brothers."

But even the universal has to find an identity of place and nationality, to find a local form and name. That is why the Poet was proud of being an Indian while aspiring to be a universal man. My father expressed the same idea in a different way when he declared that no one could be truly international unless he also was intensely national. This was true of both Gurudev and my father. For, neither of them could think of realizing the universal by escaping from his Indian identity. The Poet spoke once of finding freedom in a thousand bonds of delight. A thousand bonds of delight linked him to his motherland. His creed was one of affirmation. His greatest dreams were dreamt for his country and for his fellowmen. We must try to draw strength from the Poet who symbolized the greatest in contemplation and in achievement. We must study anew his message and learn to rise above all meanness of spirit as he would wish us to do.

§ MOHANDAS GANDHI

Broadcast over All India Radio
[New Delhi, October 1, 1968]

"In the history of India, there have been occasions when a cloud, no bigger than a man's hand, has soon covered the whole sky," so wrote Mahatma Gandhi in 1921. He himself poured life-giving water on a land thirsting for freedom.

In just four weeks in 1919, he changed the outlook of this sub-continent. He transformed the cowed and the weak into a nation which fearlessly asserted its right to be free. He gave his people a new weapon, which ultimately delivered them from colonial rule. This weapon was *satyagraha,* civil disobedience or nonviolent non-cooperation. Literally, the word means "insistence on truth." It was a weapon that did not need physical strength. But to be effective it did need the greatest self-discipline.

After Mahatma Gandhi conducted his first *satyagraha* campaigns in the country, it took India thirty long years to wrest freedom. During this time we learnt the full meaning of freedom. He taught us that a people who permitted injustice and inequality in their own society did not deserve freedom and could not preserve it. Thus equality of opportunity, irrespective of birth, sex, or religion, became the objectives of our struggle for freedom.

These ideals have come down to us through the ages, from the

Buddha, Ashoka and Akbar, to name only three of the many wise and great men who have molded our history. Mahatma Gandhi reinterpreted these old truths and applied them to our daily lives, and so made them comprehensible to the humblest of us. He forged them as instruments for a mass struggle for a peaceful political and social revolution. His stress was on reconciliation, whether amongst classes or amongst nations.

Mahatma Gandhi interpreted the yearnings of the inarticulate masses and spoke the words that they themselves were struggling to express. Wearing the loincloth, which was then all that the vast majority of our peasants could afford, he identified himself with the downtrodden and the poor. To those whom Indian society had regarded as untouchables, he gave the name "men of God," and to the last days of his life he worked ceaselessly for their uplift and emancipation. During the communal riots, this frail and aged man walked amongst the people and, through sheer faith and force of spirit, achieved miracles of reconciliation, which peace-keeping armies could not have wrought. He met his martyrdom because he refused to compromise with hatred and intolerance.

Mahatma Gandhi relied on spiritual strength. He believed in limiting one's wants and in working with one's hands. He modeled his life according to the ancient Hindu book, the Bhagavad-Gita or "the Lord's Song," but he drew inspiration also from Christianity and Islam. Indeed he thought that no man could follow his own religion truly unless he equally honored other religions. Long before him, in the third century B.C., the Emperor Ashoka had written, "In reverencing the faith of others, you will exalt your own faith and will get your own faith honored by others."

Mahatma Gandhi called his life story "My Experiments with Truth." His truth was neither exclusive nor dogmatic. As he once wrote, "There are many ways to truth, and each of us sees truth in fragment." Thus, tolerance is essential to truth; violence is incompatible with it. Nor can peace come from violence. To him, ends and means were equally important. He believed that no worthy objective could be achieved through an unworthy instrument.

Mahatma Gandhi will be remembered as a prophet and a revolutionary. He stood for resistance—nonviolent resistance—to tyranny and social injustice. He asked us to apply a test, which I quote, "Whenever you are in doubt, or when the self becomes too much with you, recall the case of the poorest and weakest man who you may have seen, and ask yourself if the step you contemplate is going to be any use to him. Will he gain anything by it? Will it restore him control over his own life and destiny? Will it lead to *swaraj,* that is self-government, for the hungry and spiritually starving millions? Then, you will find your doubts and self melting away." This test is valid for our times, indeed for all times. It is valid for India and for the world.

As long as there is oppression and degradation of the human spirit, people will seek guidance from him to assert their dignity. The weapon of nonviolent resistance which he has given mankind is today used in other lands and other climes. The world rightly regards Gandhi as the greatest Indian since the Buddha. Like the Buddha, he will continue to inspire mankind in its progress to a higher level of civilization. In India, it is our endeavor to build a future which is worthy of him.

§ JAWAHARLAL NEHRU

From address on the occasion of the first
Nehru Memorial Lecture
[New Delhi, November 14, 1967]

My father, as you all know, was the staunchest of nationalists with a deep and abiding love for India, for her traditions and for her culture. But he projected, in international assemblies and wherever he went, a new and dynamic image of India. To the downtrodden and underprivileged and the oppressed all over the world, he became the very personification of freedom, not merely freedom as the opposite of enslavement but freedom in its wider sense, that is, a liberation of the spirit. He realized fully that political freedom would always be endangered if it were not accompanied by economic regeneration and self-reliance. A perceptive historian, he was deeply conscious of the weaknesses in our society and strove relentlessly to cut asunder the old rusty chains of superstition and narrowness of mind which had isolated us from the growth of science and technology. He knew that the spirit could be liberated and free only when there was rational thinking and rational living. He felt that India could be vibrantly alive only if it could liberate its spirit. But he thought also, as indeed did Gandhiji, that no one can attain to it unless certain basic needs of the body are also met. This is why he laid so much stress on the utilization of science and technology for improving the conditions of living of our people, for widening their horizon in every way.

From address on the occasion of publication of
Homage to Nehru
[Montevideo, September 28, 1968]

All true cultures are integrative. Our great men have interpreted the ancient thought of our sages and have made it comprehensible to the common man. We in India do have a philosophical outlook on life. But it is only half the truth. We could not have built up a magnificent civilization if we had not had a well-organized material base. But it is true that Indian culture has had a great capacity to assimilate ideas and make them its own. We have learnt to create unity out of diversity.

It has been our good fortune that in time of need India has produced many great men. One such was Jawaharlal Nehru. He loved the Indian people and worked for India. Once he wrote, "If any people choose to think of me then I should like them to say: this was a man who with all his mind and heart loved India and the Indian people and they in turn were indulgent to him and gave him all their love most abundantly and extravagantly."

Yet, he was universal in spirit, and his mind and heart encompassed the whole world. One Prime Minister of Britain called Jawaharlal Nehru the first citizen of the modern world and another, Sir Winston Churchill, described him as a man who had conquered hatred and fear. Amongst his personal friends, he counted some of the best minds of his time—in science and arts and literature no less than in politics. Yet he was completely at home with the simplest peasant. I am glad to see the honor and affection in which he is held here.

§ MARTIN LUTHER KING

Address at the presentation of Jawaharlal Nehru Award for International Understanding to Mrs. Martin Luther King, Jr. [New Delhi, January 24, 1969]

This is a poignant moment for all of us. We remember vividly your last visit to our country. We had hoped that, on this occasion, Dr. King and you would be standing side by side on this platform. That was not to be. He is not with us but we feel his spirit. We admired Dr. King. We felt his loss as our own. The tragedy rekindled memories of the great martyrs of all time who gave their lives so that man might live and grow. We thought of the great men in your own country who fell to the assassin's bullet and of Mahatma Gandhi's martyrdom here in this city, this very month, twenty-one years ago. Such events remain as wounds in the human consciousness, reminding us of battles yet to be fought and tasks still to be accomplished. We should not mourn for men of high ideals. Rather we should rejoice that we had the privilege of having had them with us, to inspire us by their radiant personalities. So today we are gathered not to offer you grief, but to salute a man who achieved so much in so short a time. It is befitting, Madam, that you whom he called the "courage by my side," you who gave him strength and encouragement in his historic mission, should be with us to receive this award.

You and your husband both had foreseen that death might come to him violently. It was perhaps inherent in the situation. Dr. King chose death for the theme of a sermon, remarking that he would like to be remembered as a drum major for justice, for peace and for righteousness. When you were once asked what you would do if your husband were assassinated, you were courage personified, replying that you might weep but the work would go on. Your face of sorrow, so beautiful in its dignity coupled with infinite compassion, will forever be engraved in our hearts.

Mahatma Gandhi also had foreseen his end and had prepared himself for it. Just as training for violence included learning to kill, the training for nonviolence, he said, included learning how to die. The true badge of the *satyagrahi* is to be unafraid.

As if he too had envisaged the martyrdoms of Mahatma Gandhi and Martin Luther King, Rabindranath Tagore once sang:

> *In anger we slew him,*
> *With love let us embrace him now,*
> *For in death he lives again amongst us,*
> *The mighty conqueror of death.*

This award, Madam, is the highest tribute our nation can bestow on work for understanding and brotherhood among men. It is named after a man who himself was a peacemaker and who all his life labored passionately for freedom, justice and peace in India and throughout the world. Dr. Martin Luther King's struggle was for these same values. He paid for his ideals with his blood, forging a new bond among the brave and the conscientious of all races and all nations.

Dr. King's dream embraced the poor and the oppressed of all lands. His work ennobled us. He spoke of the right of man to survive and recognized three threats to the survival of man—racial injustice, poverty and war. He realized that even under the lamp of affluence which was held aloft by science, lay the shadow of poverty, compelling two-thirds of the peoples of the world to exist in hunger and want. He proclaimed that mankind could be saved from war only if we cared enough for peace to sacrifice for it.

Dr. Martin Luther King drew his inspiration from Christ, and his method of action from Mahatma Gandhi. Only through truth can untruth be vanquished. Only through love can hatred be quenched. This is the path of the Buddha and of Christ, and in our own times, that of Mahatma Gandhi and of Martin Luther King.

They believed in the equality of all men. No more false doctrine has been spread than that of the superiority of one race over another. It is ironical that there should still be people in this world who judge men not by their moral worth and intellectual merit but by the pigment of their skin or other physical characteristics.

Some governments still rest on the theory of racist superiority—such as the governments of South Africa and the lawless regime in Rhodesia. Unregenerate groups in other countries consider one color superior to another. Our own battle is not yet over. Caste and other prejudices still survive, but most of us are ashamed of them and recognize them as evils to be combated. We are trying hard to eradicate them.

While there is bondage anywhere, we ourselves cannot be fully free. While there is oppression anywhere, we ourselves cannot soar high. Martin Luther King was convinced that one day the misguided people who believed in racial superiority would realize the error of their ways. His dream was that white and black, brown and yellow would live and grow together as flowers in a garden with their faces turned towards the sun. As you yourself said, "All of us who believe in what Martin Luther King stood for, must see to it that his spirit never dies." That spirit can never die. There may be setbacks in our fight for the equality of all men. There may be moments of gloom. But victory must and will be ours. Let us not rest until the equality of all races and religions becomes a living fact. That is the most effective and lasting tribute that we can pay to Dr. King.

Index